NATIONAL SYMBOLS
of
ST. MARTIN

A PRIMER

BOOKS BY
HOUSE OF NEHESI PUBLISHERS

COMING, COMING HOME:
CONVERSATIONS II
by George Lamming

IN SEARCH OF ST. MARTIN'S
ANCIENT PEOPLES –
PREHISTORIC ARCHAEOLOGY
by Dr. Jay B. Haviser

MORE THAN A DREAM –
PRESCRIPTIONS FOR SUCCESS
by Jackson C. Stevens, Ph.D.
with Asha Stevens-Mohabier, M.Ed.

IMAGES OF ME
by Ingrid Zagers

ILLEGAL TRUTH
by Ras Changa

QUIMBÉ – THE POETICS OF
SOUND
by Lasana M. Sekou

MOTHERNATION – POEMS FROM
1984 TO 1987
by Lasana M. Sekou

THE INDEPENDENCE PAPERS –
READINGS ON A NEW POLITICAL
STATUS FOR ST. MAARTEN/
ST. MARTIN, VOLUME 1
eds. Lasana M. Sekou,
Oswald Francis, Napolina Gumbs

GOLDEN VOICES OF S'MAATIN
by Ruby Bute

LOVE SONGS MAKE YOU CRY
by Lasana M. Sekou

NATIVITY & DRAMATIC
MONOLOGUES FOR TODAY
by Lasana M. Sekou

MASQUERADE
by Ian Valz

BORN HERE
by Lasana M. Sekou

MAROON LIVES – A TRIBUTE TO
GRENADIAN FREEDOM FIGHTERS
by Lasana M. Sekou

IMAGES IN THE YARD
by Lasana M. Sekou

FOR THE MIGHTY GODS ...
AN OFFERING
by Lasana M. Sekou

MOODS FOR ISIS ...
PICTUREPOEMS OF LOVE &
STRUGGLE
by Lasana M. Sekou

NATIONAL SYMBOLS
of
ST. MARTIN

A PRIMER

EDITED BY LASANA M. SEKOU

HOUSE OF NEHESI PUBLISHERS • ST MARTIN, CARIBBEAN

HOUSE OF NEHESI PUBLISHERS
P. O. Box 222
Philipsburg, St. Martin
Caribbean

Second edition Copyright © 1996 by Lasana M. Sekou (H. H. Lake).
First edition Copyright © 1990 by House of Nehesi Publishers.
ISBN: 0-913441-18-X
Library of Congress Cat. No: 94-76966

ALL RIGHTS RESERVED. No part of this book may be reproduced or transmitted in any form or by any means, electronic or mechanical, including photocopying, recording, or by any information storage and retrieval system, without permission in writing from the Publisher and Editor.

Editorial Assistant: Rhoda Arrindell

Book design by Blackboard: Cozbi Sanchez-Cabrera
Michelle Smith
James C. Best, Jr.

Illustrations: David Kobelt
Pham Son
Cozbi Sanchez-Cabrera
Roland Richardson
Edward Glascow
Ruby Bute
Frans de Kock
Gary G. Jefferson

Cover Graphics Design: Carole Maugé-Lewis

Cover Photography: P. Gunn, W. Roumou, SSC

Cover Painting: Roland Richardson, *Philipsburg Flamboyant*, oil.

ACKNOWLEDGMENT

STINAPA reports reprinted and adapted with permission from STINAPA-Sint Maarten. Maps of St. Martin reprinted with permission from the Caribbean Conservation Association. Much thanks to Tovia Burroughs; proof-readers Connie Francis, Joyce Peters-McKenzie, Jacqueline Sample, and Joy Reiph; Sixto Peters/Dutch translations; J. H. Lake, Jr./*Newsday*; Beverly Wilson; Eddie Bobo; Daniella Jeffry; Ingrid Brandt/Francia Housen/Blanca Hodge/Philipsburg Jubilee Library; Senator Will Johnson; R. Galmeijer/Mr. Eleanora/Postal Service; Maritsa A. James-Christina/Harold Bosnie/Court Recorder; Alberto Mathew/Joshua Bell/Census Office; Elsje Wilson/Sint Maarten Museum; Dr. A. Scott; Mabel Scott; Alex Reiph; Alex Richards/Municipal Library; Roland Duncan; Delta Dorsch; Clarence "Cherra" Heyliger; Rufus Vanderpool; Alexis Christmas-Secretary; St. Patrick's Church (St. Croix); Lynne Hinkey-MacDonald, marine advisor; Janice Hodge; Dianne Richardson; Gumbs & Associates; Mobutu Illidge; Marianne Illidge; Marie-Line Hughes-Richards/The Mairie; Harold Arnell; Mercedes de Coste; Lorenzo Duruo; Myron Chenault; Percy Cox; Leo Friday; Romeo Pantophlet/Central Bureau of Statistics; Ashford James/Meteorological Service; Roland Trompert/Cadastre; Rupert Maynard; Ronald Peterson; Rita Peterson; Roland Richardson/*Discover St. Martin-St. Maarten*; Thomassillienne Arnell; Mayor Albert Fleming; Zoila Meran; Ruby Wilkes; Ijahnya Christian; Wilfred Roumou; Janice James; N. Richardson; Judith Tjin A Sioe; Algemeen Rijksarchief; Don Hughes/PJD-2; Alex Choisy; Guavaberry & Liqueur Co.; Plan'D2; Greenfingers; Butterfly Farm; Susan; Maxime Larmonie/Ron Daal/Cede-St. Martin.

For Nzinga ...

Sovereignty is not possible where the majority are excluded from this process of the collective control of agendas and continuing self-definition.

– GEORGE LAMMING

MAPS/CHARTS/CHRONOLOGIES

CHRONOLOGY OF THE NATIONAL FLAG
page 8

PONDS OF ST. MARTIN
page 107

ST. MARTIN MARINE HABITATS
page 12

SALT PRODUCTION, 1849-1850
page 114

CHRONOLOGIE – LE SEL À SAINT MARTIN (1789-1961)
page 117

GREAT SALT POND
page 120

ST. MARTIN TERRESTRIAL LIFE ZONES
page 123

ST. MARTIN MARINE RESOURCES USE
page 125

ST. MARTIN NATURAL ATTRACTIONS
page 126

ISLETS AND KEYS OF ST. MARTIN
page 132

MORE BIRDS OF ST. MARTIN
page 137

ST. MARTIN ENDANGERED AND LOCALLY IMPORTANT SPECIES
page 138

SIMPSON BAY LAGOON
page 151

FORT WILLEM, FORT AMSTERDAM
page 154

A CHRONOLOGY OF ST. MARTIN'S FORTS
page 158

ELEVATION AND DEPTH CONTOUR
page 160

MAP OF THE CARIBBEAN
page 162

CONTENTS

vi   MAPS/CHARTS/CHRONOLOGIES
ix   PREFACE

CHAPTER I

IN THE FORGE OF A NATIONAL IDENTITY

3   ISLAND-NATION
4   NATIONAL MOTTO
4   NATIONAL FLAG EMBLEM
5   NATIONAL FLAG
8   CHRONOLOGY OF THE NATIONAL FLAG
14   IN SALUTE TO OUR FLAG
15   NATIONAL FLOWERS
15   NATIONAL TREE
15   NATIONAL BIRD
15   PATRIOTIC AND POPULAR SONGS
15   NATIONAL DANCE
15   NATIONAL DAYS/FESTIVALS
16   NATIONAL MONUMENTS AND RESERVES
16   NATIONAL DISHES
16   NATIONAL DRINK
16   POPULAR SOUPS
16   POPULAR DRINKS AND LIQUEURS
17   POPULAR DESSERTS AND TRADITIONAL SWEETS
17   TRADITIONAL JELLIES, JAMS, AND PRESERVES
17   POPULAR AND TRADITIONAL BREADS
17   POPULAR FRUITS
18   THE CREATIVE WORD

CHAPTER II

FACES OF THE PEOPLE

Forerunners of St. Martin's Freedom

29   MAROONS AND ST. MARTIN
35   THE REVOLT AND MASSACRE OF 1830
38   ONE-TÉTÉ LOHKAY
40   ST. MARTIN'S EMANCIPATION OF 1848
45   DIAMOND ESTATE 26

Profiles of St. Martiners in History

49   INEZ ELIZA BALY-LEWIS
51   ANTHONY REYNIER BROUWER
56   FELIX CHOISY
60   CARLOS ALEXANDER COOKS
63   THOMAS EMMANUEL DURUO
68   MELFORD AUGUSTUS HAZEL
70   JOSEPH HUSURELL LAKE, SR.
78   NINA LARMONIE-DUVERLY
79   FRANCOIS AUGUSTE PERRINON
81   ALRETT BERTRAUND PETERS
83   WALLACE BRADFORD PETERSON
86   ALBERIC ÁURELIEN RICHARDS
90   MARIE RICHARDS
93   LEONIDES RICHARDSON
95   LIONEL BERNARD SCOTT
100   SIMEONE VENTER-TROTT
102   PAUL ANTONIN WHIT, SR.

CHAPTER III

THE NATURE OF ST. MARTIN

107	Ponds of St. Martin
108	The Great Salt Pond
110	A Historical Overview
110	Salt and Salt Ponds
121	Birds of the Pond
122	The Freshwater Lobster
122	Pond Vegetation
124	Simpson Bay Lagoon
126	Beaches of St. Martin
130	Beach Plants
132	Beach Birds
132	Islets and Keys of St. Martin
133	The Brown Pelican – National Bird of St. Martin
137	More Birds of St. Martin
138	Trees as Cultural Monuments
139	Guavaberry Tree
140	Tamarind Tree
142	Plant a Tree
145	Sugar Plantations of Marigot
155	Forts of St. Martin
158	A Chronology of St. Martin's Forts
160	Highest Hills
163	Bibliography
170	Index

PREFACE

St. Martin[1] is at a crossroads in her history. It is time for visioned, courageous, and activist men and women, young and old, to harvest the winds of democratic change blowing across the world. These resilient winds of democratic change are fanning the consciousness of St. Martiners toward fully developing and transforming our identity, progressive ideas, and informed nation building activities as one people, one nation, with one destiny.

The "One People" are the people of the island's North and South, incorrectly called "Frenchside" and "Dutchside." "Frenchside" and "Dutchside" are colonial codes or designations which claim St. Martin for the Republic of France and the Kingdom of The Netherlands, instead of for the island's people. Indeed, the labor and love, blood and tears, hopes and dreams of the St. Martin people have given birth to a national consciousness. This consciousness is generating our unique destiny as a Caribbean nation. The "One Nation" is the indivisible people and land mass, keys, and islets of St. Martin.

The "One Destiny" is our National Destiny as a sovereign people. Our National Destiny is the political re-unification of St. Martin, fused with the social, familial, and cultural unity and the customs free/duty-free economic "common market"—in the making since 1648, and engaged by the majority of St. Martiners since 1848. In achieving our National Destiny, which can only be democratically prepared for and constructed, lies our fullest sense of nationhood and prosperity.

Toward the building and realization of genuine nationhood, a people need their "national" symbols (people, places, ideas, products, events, movements) for individual inspiration and around which to rally collectively. National symbols are ideas, images, and activities which are integral to identifying the people's unique history (including heroes, heroines, nation builders, historic events, positive social/family values, ideals, language, multilingual aptitude, cultural creations, political culture). National symbols also condition and are conditioned by current realities and provide an inexhaustible reservoir from which the people can equip themselves to better determine their future. Within this context, the Flag, which stands for the entire nation, is universally the most important, visible, embracing, and stirring national symbol.

This book, headlining the National Flag of St. Martin, was conceived in the critical womb of St. Martin people's material, cultural, and spiritual experiences. It was weaned by the people's expressed need to "Know Thyself." *National Symbols of St. Martin – A Primer* records, highlights, and proposes regenerative features of the composite face of St. Martin's natural, popular, and national symbols. These symbols exist naturally, historically, and/or culturally in the heart, mind, soul, and actions of the St. Martiner. This book is by no means exhaustive of what we have, who we are, and where we are going. It is but a basic composition, reflective of the core of St. Martin's cultural dynamism.

The *National Symbols of St. Martin* is but a catalysis for further research into the core and continuum of the St. Martin Experience. Sound and critical knowledge of the St. Martin Experience is essential for the formal and informal passing on of sound family values and elevating spiritual ideals; the progressive construction of independent nationhood; the protection of and harmonization with our natural environment; the democratic advancement of our national culture; our confident and productive participation in the global village; claiming the responsibility and reaping the rewards of justice, freedom, democracy, and economic prosperity as proud men and women, subject to no colonial authority; the enabling of every St. Martiner to invest freely, courageously, and with an informed passion in forging a culture of victory.

When vibrantly and creatively engaged, national symbols are indispensable to addressing and embracing the multi-cultural interaction and cross-fertilization potential and practices going on in this country. Such symbols are elemental to a holistic education system that would liberate St. Martin, as a country, triumphantly into the twenty-first century. This education system would succeed in our best individual and national interest once developed by informed, progressive, confident St. Martiners and implemented in all of our schools for a more integrated, independent, united, and successful St. Martin.

— LASANA M. SEKOU
St. Martin, 1996

[1] *St. Martin refers to the entire island, unless otherwise indicated.*

Etching: "The Silk Cotton Tree," by Roland Richardson.

Chapter 1

In The Forge of a National Identity

And now, now they try
to study the past

and tell each other—
"you remember when"

and ask each other—
"you remember how?"

And some who don't know
anything at all about S'maatin,
shorten her history just in
johnny cakes and fish

— RUBY BUTE
Bring Forth Children

ISLAND-NATION:	**St. Martin**
ANCIENT NAMES:	Sualouiga, Öualichi (Sualouiga, also pronounced and written Souliaga or Soualiga, is thought to be an Island Carib word meaning "Land of Salt." Öualichi, also pronounced and written Qualichi, is said to be an Arawakan word meaning "Land of Women" or "Land of Brave Women.")
LOCATION:	18.20 degrees N. latitude and 63.07 degrees W. longitude
SIZE:	37 square miles (Not including islets and keys)
POPULATION:	70,000 (Unofficial 1996 est.); 81,978 (1995 est., South – 28,940; North – 28,524; Est. unregistered immigrant pop. – 24,514)[2]
MAJOR GEOGRAPHIC DIVISIONS:	South, 16 square miles; North, 21 square miles
CAPITALS:	Great Bay (Philipsburg) in the South; Marigot in the North
NICKNAMES:	The Rock, Friendly Island, Sunshine City, Sweet St. Martin

---

[2]*Source: Central Bureau of Statistics, April 1994 (Netherlands Antilles); Statistical Department 1992 Census (Guadeloupe). CBS's official count of unregistered persons in the South in 1994 was 10,514. Mairie's officials estimated the number of unregistered immigrants in the North to have been 14,000 in 1993. The island's population decreased due to forced deportation and emigration in the aftermath of Hurricane Luis. The cyclone struck the island with over 120 m.p.h. gusts on September 5, 1995.*

NATIONAL MOTTO

"The Gale Doesn't Stop At The Frontier."

Origin and meaning: The National Motto is a traditional and philosophical St. Martin "saying," born out of the people's historical, material, and socio-cultural experiences and aspirations to succeed as a united nation. The National Motto expresses the fundamental understanding and belief in the unity and "national character" of the land and people of St. Martin. The National Motto acknowledges and declares explicitly, from an independent and native perspective, that whatever happens (whether for bad or good) in any one part of St. Martin will invariably and significantly affect the entire island-nation. This traditional saying implies that the destiny of St. Martin and her people, from the North and South, are inextricably linked. The National Motto informs successive generations that each and every St. Martiner is inherently committed to knowing, informing, and sharing the progressive and mutually-beneficial principles, practices, and spirit of peaceful coexistence, fraternity, love, hospitality, freedom, democracy, self-reliance, and national advancement.

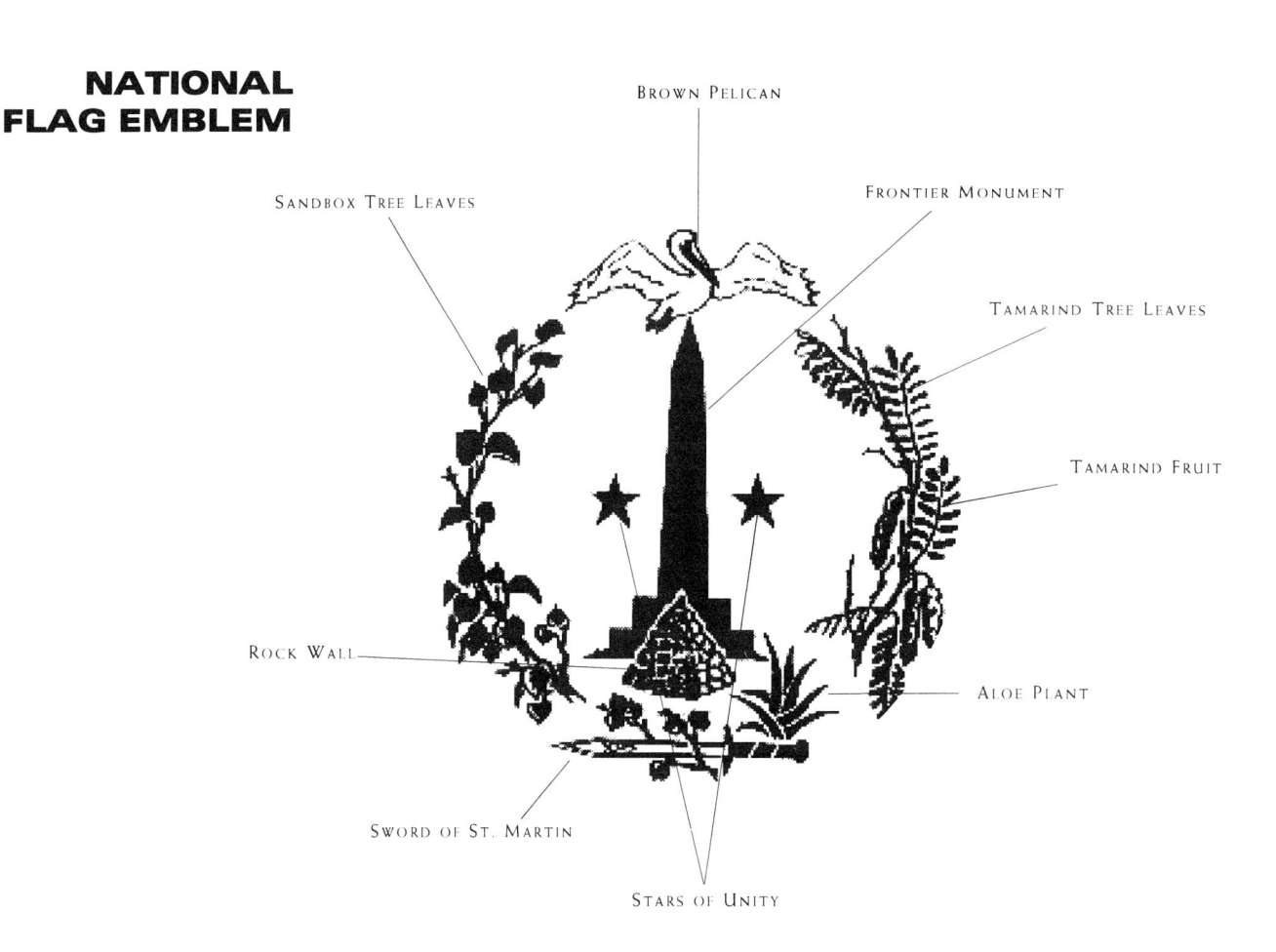

NATIONAL FLAG EMBLEM

Labels:
- Brown Pelican
- Sandbox Tree Leaves
- Frontier Monument
- Tamarind Tree Leaves
- Tamarind Fruit
- Rock Wall
- Aloe Plant
- Sword of St. Martin
- Stars of Unity

NATIONAL FLAG

The National Flag of St. Martin (North and South), unveiled on August 31, 1990, is designed to represent both parts or sides of the island and her people as one nation. The National Flag is now being used in a variety of ways by the people of St. Martin as a concrete socio-cultural symbol that embodies the history and hopes, the labor and love, the tribulations and triumphs, the unity and strength, ideals and progress of the St. Martin people.

The "meaning" of the colors

The colors of the National Flag of St. Martin are green, medium blue, red, light blue, yellow, and black.

Green represents the fertile and beautiful land of St. Martin that sustains our people. Green also represents the succession lands which are fundamental to St. Martin's core socio-cultural values. Green is the foundation color bar of the National Flag. It "means" that through individual initiative and by working together, in mutual respect, by the guiding light of liberty, the nurturing bonds of brotherhood, and undying love for the land, the people of St. Martin will achieve democracy, equality, justice, peace, independence, greater unity, and prosperity.

Blue (medium) represents the sea that surrounds us with abundant life and is one of our prime natural resources. Medium blue is the second color bar of the National Flag. It "means" that St. Martiners should strive to be as strong and resourceful as the sea and live the power of truth—as the "waves of the sea," philosophically, represent righteousness and the diffusion of spiritual truth over the land.

Red (warm) represents the noble blood of our people—past, present, and future. Red is the National Flag's third successive color bar in ascending order. It "means" that our people's blood runs strong, deep, proud, rich, and eternal as the sea.

Blue (light) symbolizes the vast sky as it relates to the positive and boundless activities and potential that grow from the people. Blue is the fourth ascending color bar. It "means" that our people must aspire to achieve the highest in personal, familial, and national development and international solidarity and peaceful coexistence, with the proverbial sky as the only limit.

Yellow symbolizes the regenerative energy of the sun. Yellow is the top color bar. It "means" that the life-generating victories realized, and to be realized through the help and blessing of

God and the resiliency of St. Martin's people, will guide us consciously and continually to an ever brighter and prosperous future which we must all work for together.

The Emblem

The Emblem in the canton (upper left hand corner on the yellow bar when facing the National Flag) symbolizes the historical, social, and cultural unity of the people and land of St. Martin. The symbols in the canton are illustrated in black. **Black**, for the National Flag, signifies the striving for spiritual perfection within and the striving for harmony with humanity and nature.

The central unification symbol is the **Frontier Monument** (an obelisk), born out of the people's belief and maintenance of our island as one nation.

Our people's labor during the unholy slave period and our subsequent building of St. Martin, while continually attaining our freedom, is symbolized by a pyramid-shaped outcropping of **Rock Wall**. The pyramid is patterned after the shape of harvested salt ("salt heaps") when salt-picking was consistently the island's single most industry before and after 1848, and refers to the people's labor being the "Salt of the Land." The rocks symbolize strength and building; they also "mark" the first set of stones piled by our ancestors on the spot where the Treaty of Concordia was signed in 1648, peacefully "partitioning" the island and laying the groundwork for coexistence as one people.

The symbols of unity through labor are flanked by two **Stars**, representing the unity of the people from the North and South of St. Martin.

At the foundation of the National Flag's Emblem is the "**Sword of St. Martin**," symbolizing defense of country and justice for all. The legend of the fourth century soldier/bishop Martin, from whom the island got her current name, tearing his soldier's cloak in half to give part as clothing to a poor man—an act which is invariably expressed in the noble hospitality St. Martiners traditionally show to others from a position of confidence and fairness—is implied.

Above the sword's hilt is the **Aloe Plant**, a symbol of healing and curing, of internal and external ailments. The aloe plant in this position signifies that a nation must continually strive to heal its people through the administration of justice.

The sword's blade is sheathed, as a counter balance and as a sign of peace and friendship, by the leaves of the **Sandbox Tree**. The Sandbox tree is a traditional symbol of wisdom. Under this tree, folk-tales, proverbs, family, social, and "national" views and histories; cultural manifestations; and values of love were passed down from one generation to the next. Therefore, the sword of defense and justice is tempered by wisdom and motivated by the free will to defend, share fairly, and heal.

The Sandbox leaves (left side) and the **Tamarind leaves and Fruit** (right side) encircle the center symbols of unity, labor, peoplehood, justice, and healing. The tamarind tree was sacred to the enslaved ancestors because of the shade it provided from the sun's scorching heat. Today it remains a pride of St. Martin's trees. The tamarind fruit represents for the National Flag the bitter-sweet realities of life. It is through these realities that St. Martiners must endure, with the strength of this tree, fruitful and diverse in our productivity as the fruit and leaves of the tamarind tree.

The crowning glory of the Emblem is the **Brown Pelican** in flight. The Brown Pelican is St. Martin's national bird and is facing east on the National Flag. The pelican symbolizes grace, resourcefulness, courage, and sacrifice. It is said that during times of hardship, this noble and courageous bird will tear open its breast with its beak and feed its young on its own blood—meaning that the pelican will sacrifice its life by any means necessary so that the young, the future, will be provided with an opportunity to live.

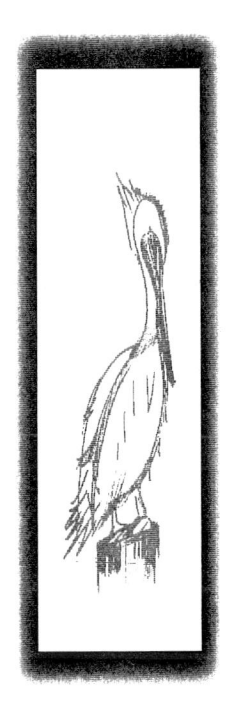

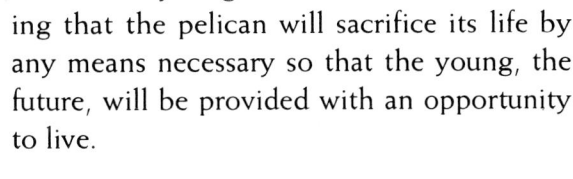

BROWN PELICAN

CHRONOLOGY OF THE NATIONAL FLAG

(AUGUST 31) NATIONAL FLAG OF ST. MARTIN IS UNVEILED BY AD-HOC INFORMATION COMMITTEE ON NATIONAL SYMBOLS (ICONS), FOLLOWING "PRELIMINARY CONFERENCE ON NATIONAL SYMBOLS" AT PHILIPSBURG JUBILEE LIBRARY. FIRST EDITION OF *NATIONAL SYMBOLS OF ST. MARTIN - A PRIMER* IS PUBLISHED AS CONFERENCE'S COMPANION BOOKLET. POLITICAL LEADERS AND ACTIVISTS ARE AMONG AUDIENCE THAT ATTENDS UNVEILING, AND EXPRESS SUPPORT FOR THE "PROPOSED" FLAG REPRESENTING THE PEOPLE AND ISLAND OF "ST. MAARTEN/ST. MARTIN." FLAG BUTTONS ARE PURCHASED.
←1990

(SEPTEMBER 5) MANY MORE PEOPLE SEE THE "PROPOSED" NATIONAL FLAG FOR FIRST TIME IN A COLOR PICTORIAL OF THE UNVEILING IN *ST. MAARTEN/ST. MARTIN NEWSDAY*.
←1990

(NOVEMBER 11) NATIONAL FLAG ON COVER OF *THE INDEPENDENCE PAPERS - READINGS ON A NEW POLITICAL STATUS FOR ST. MAARTEN/ST. MARTIN, VOL. 1*, THE ISLAND'S FIRST COMPILATION OF POLITICAL WRITINGS.
←1990

(NOVEMBER 12) NATIONAL FLAG IS CARRIED BY ST. MARTIN EDUCATIONAL AND CULTURAL ORGANIZATION IN FIRST UNITY DAY RALLY ORGANIZED BY MUNICIPAL GOVERNMENT IN MARIGOT. OVER 2000 PERSONS TAKE PART. HUNDREDS WEAR NATIONAL FLAG BUTTONS AND STICK DECALS TO THEIR BARE CHESTS, SHIRTS, AND BLOUSES, AS THEY MARCH THROUGH MARIGOT TO THE ALBERIC RICHARDS STADIUM.
←1990

(DECEMBER) OVER 1000 NATIONAL FLAG DECALS DISTRIBUTED. NOW SEEN ON TAXIS, BUSES, RENTAL CARS, AND OTHER VEHICLES. DECALS ARE SEEN ON FRONT DOOR OF HOMES AND BUSINESSES.
←1990

(**February**)
National Flag raised for first time on house rafter, a custom to signal that builders have reached the highest point of construction. The house, in French Quarter, belongs to social worker and politician Jeanine Arnell.

←1991

(**March**)
National Flag flown in St. Martin's annual Heineken Regatta on the "Magdalentje," belonging to environmentalist Francois van der Hoeven.

←1991

(**April**)
National Reformation Party, founded by attorney and businessman, Richard Gibson, raises National Flag at NRP's headquarters during Island Council election in South of St. Martin. St. Maarten Patriotic Alliance candidate Leonard Priest poses with Flag in television campaign advertisement.

←1991

(**August** 31)
First anniversary of National Flag observed with well-attended poetry recital at Orleans Cultural Center. Sir Gaston Boasman delivers feature address.

←1991

(**November** 3)
Emblem of National Flag appears as "logo" for citizens action group, People Committed to Inform (PCTI), during its introductory forum, "Port de Plaisance and the road to the future development of St. Maarten/St. Martin."

←1991

(NOVEMBER 6) IN ST. MARTIN DAY ADDRESS TO THE CURACAO-BASED ST. MAARTEN CULTURAL FOUNDATION, CAMILLE BALY, CULTURAL ADVISOR TO THE GOVERNMENT IN GREAT BAY, ACKNOWLEDGES NATIONAL FLAG AS A TRUE SYMBOL OF ST. MARTIN'S PEOPLE AND CALLS IT "THE CULTURAL FLAG." BY THIS TIME, THE BANNER IS ALSO BEING CALLED "THE UNITY FLAG" AND "THE PEOPLE'S FLAG." BALY'S ADDRESS, "SIMARTN - A PEOPLE'S HISTORY IN CULTURAL PERSPECTIVE," IS DELIVERED AT THE UNIVERSITY OF THE NETHERLANDS ANTILLES (UNA).

~1991

(NOVEMBER 7) ICONS MEMBERS LASANA M. SEKOU AND HORACE WHIT FORMALLY PRESENT THE NATIONAL FLAG TO MAYOR ALBERT FLEMING AT MAIRIE IN MARIGOT. FLEMING, WHILE RECEIVING FLAG DECALS AND BUTTONS, SAYS THAT HE HOPES "ALL THE PEOPLE OF ST. MARTIN WILL BE PROUD TO FLY THE NATIONAL FLAG."

~1991

(NOVEMBER) NATIONAL FLAG BORNE IN PRO-NEW STATUS UNITY DAY RALLY IN MARIGOT.

~1991

(APRIL) NATIONAL FLAG FLIES FOR FIRST TIME IN CARNIVAL VILLAGE AS PART OF TAMARA LEONARD'S TALENT SEGMENT IN PJD-2'S CARIBBEAN QUEEN PAGEANT. LEONARD, A HIGH SCHOOL STUDENT, EMERGES AS THE PAGEANT'S WINNER.

~1992

(AUGUST) SECOND ANNIVERSARY OF NATIONAL FLAG OBSERVED WITH SPECIAL PROGRAM BY ALEX REIPH FOR "CONSCIOUS LYRICS" PROGRAM ON RADIO ST. MARTIN.

~1992

CONSENSUS, THE INDEPENDENT COMMITTEE WHICH DEVELOPED HISTORIC PROPOSAL FOR NORTHERN ST. MARTIN'S POLITICAL/FISCAL AUTONOMY, PRODUCES T-SHIRT WITH NATIONAL FLAG COLORS.

←1992

(**DECEMBER**) JEWELRY-QUALITY FLAG LAPEL PINS AVAILABLE.

←1992

(**DECEMBER** 19) NATIONAL FLAG IS HOISTED AT WEDDING RECEPTION OF FRANKLYN HODGE AND ENA HODGE-BOASMAN, AT HOME OF BRIDE'S FATHER IN FRENCH QUARTER.

←1992

(**FEBRUARY** 23-26) AT REQUEST OF ST. MARTIN/ANTILLEAN STUDENT ORGANIZATION, AN EXHIBIT OF NATIONAL FLAG IS SET UP AT UNIVERSITY OF VIRGIN ISLANDS DURING THE ORGANIZATION'S INTRODUCTORY CONFERENCE.

←1993

(**FEBRUARY-MARCH**) NATIONAL FLAG IS RAISED AT LA SAVANNE SPORTS PARK FOR NORTH-SOUTH VOLLEYBALL TOURNAMENT, HOSTED BY YOUTHS VOLLEYBALL CLUB. THE NATIONAL FLAG OF ST. MARTIN, FLANKED BY THE FLAGS OF THE NETHERLANDS AND FRANCE, REMAINS FLYING FOR DURATION OF TOURNAMENT.

←1993

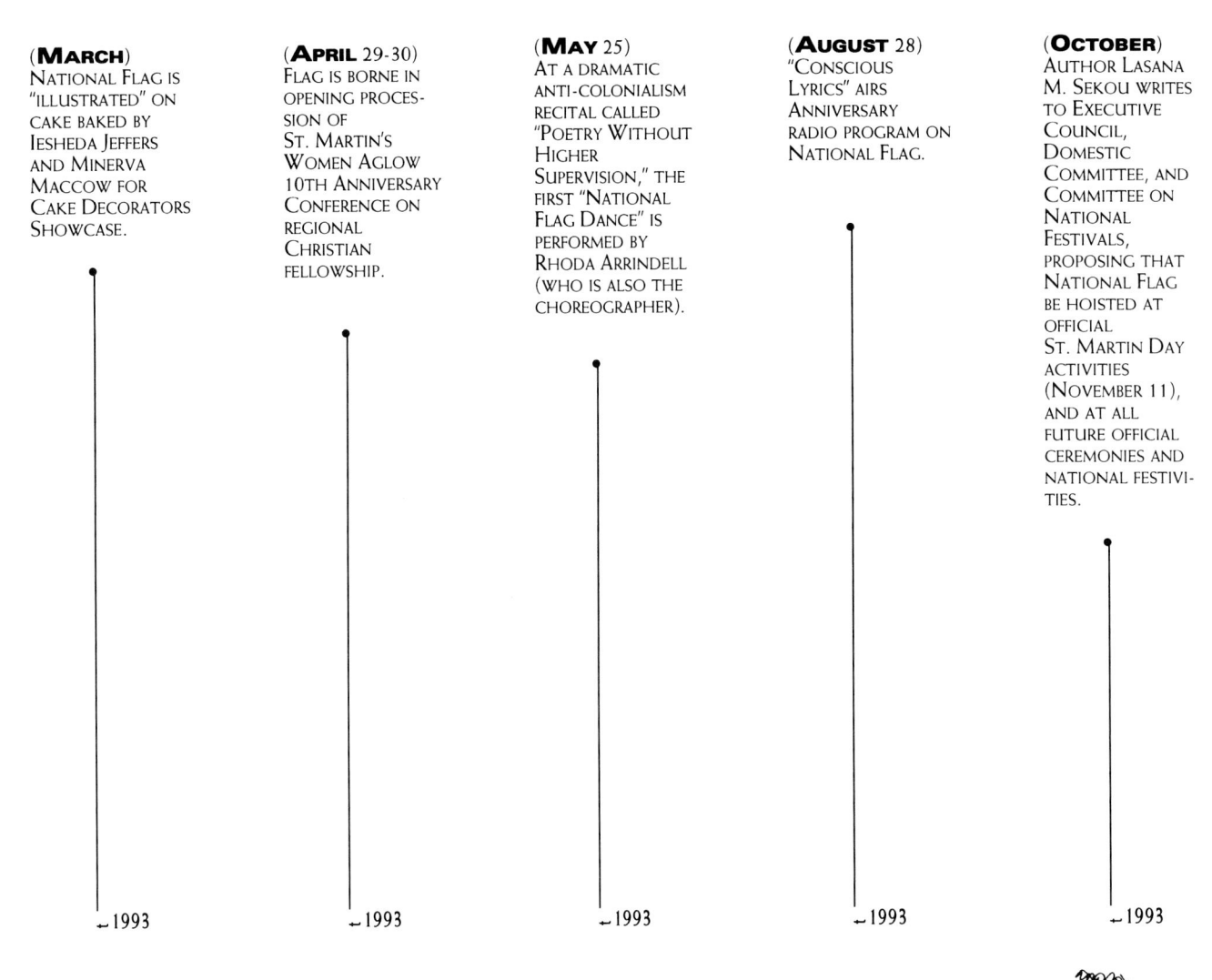

(March)
National Flag is "illustrated" on cake baked by Iesheda Jeffers and Minerva Maccow for Cake Decorators Showcase.

—1993

(April 29-30)
Flag is borne in opening procession of St. Martin's Women Aglow 10th Anniversary Conference on regional Christian fellowship.

—1993

(May 25)
At a dramatic anti-colonialism recital called "Poetry Without Higher Supervision," the first "National Flag Dance" is performed by Rhoda Arrindell (who is also the choreographer).

—1993

(August 28)
"Conscious Lyrics" airs Anniversary radio program on National Flag.

—1993

(October)
Author Lasana M. Sekou writes to Executive Council, Domestic Committee, and Committee on National Festivals, proposing that National Flag be hoisted at official St. Martin Day activities (November 11), and at all future official ceremonies and national festivities.

—1993

(**OCTOBER** 27) NATIONAL FLAG AND SEKOU'S LETTER DISCUSSED BY DOMESTIC COMMITTEE (BODY OF ALL ELECTED ISLAND COUNCILORS IN GREAT BAY).

—1993

(**NOVEMBER**) OFFICIAL ST. MARTIN DAY ACTIVITIES CANCELLED AFTER LOBBYING EFFORTS OF THE AD-HOC SOLIDARITY COMMITTEE PROTESTING ARREST OF GOVERNMENT LEADER CLAUDE WATHEY IN CONNECTION WITH PRINCESS JULIANA INTERNATIONAL AIRPORT EXPANSION SCANDAL. SOME SOLIDARITY MEMBERS ASK FOR NATIONAL FLAG TO BE FLOWN AS AN ANTI-COLONIAL PROTEST. AT ONE POINT THE DUTCH FLAG IS REMOVED FROM FLAG POLE IN FRONT OF GOVERNMENT ADMINISTRATION BUILDING.

—1993

(**AUGUST** 31) ON ANNIVERSARY OF NATIONAL FLAG, THE INDEPENDENCE FOR ST. MARTIN FOUNDATION IS LAUNCHED TO CHAMPION INDEPENDENCE OPTION IN "ST. MAARTEN REFERENDUM" OF OCTOBER 14, 1994. ISM MEMBERS WEAR NATIONAL FLAG LAPEL PINS AT FIRST PRESS CONFERENCE. NATIONAL FLAG ADORNS ISM'S OFFICE.

—1994

WILLIAM MARLIN, THEN COMMISSIONER OF EDUCATION & CULTURE, PROPOSES MEETING WITH MUNICIPAL GOVERNMENT ON JOINT USE OF NATIONAL FLAG. FLAG ON EXHIBIT IN ST. MARTIN BOOTH AT CARIFESTA VI.

t 1995

(**APRIL** 22) *CHAMPION* EDITOR LEOPOLD JAMES AND ILS LABOR LEADER ELDRIDGE VAN PUTTEN PROTEST DUTCH WINDMILL AND FRANCE'S EIFFEL TOWER ICONS ON CARNIVAL WELCOMING POSTER AT SUALOUIGA ROAD, BY SPRAY-PAINTING AN "X" OVER ICONS. BOTH SAY ICONS REPRESENTATIVE OF COLONIAL COUNTRIES, NOT ST. MARTIN PEOPLE AND CARIBBEAN CULTURE. BEFORE BEING ARRESTED, BOTH MEN RAISE NATIONAL FLAG AT SITE, CALLING FLAG THE TRUE REPRESENTATION OF ST. MARTIN'S HISTORY AND CULTURE. FLAG REMOVED BY UNKNOWN PERSON. PROTESTERS HOLD CARNIVAL DEVELOPMENT FOUNDATION RESPONSIBLE FOR MISSING FLAG.

• 1996

IN SALUTE TO OUR FLAG

By Danny Hassell

We have taken so much for granted
Even this Land where our roots are planted
This Land where past generations toiled
While giving each other a helping hand

Then progress came and over the years
It caused us oh so many tears
But a friend[3] came along one day
With a song to wipe our tears away
To impress in us as we grow
That the best prize in hand
Was our Sweet St. Martin Land

And today a refrain in union we may sing
For a new banner of Nation hails in the high wind
It is thy Flag of Unity, let it fly
So that the seeds of division may die.

[3] *G. Kemps, author of "O Sweet St. Martin Land."*

NATIONAL FLOWERS:	Yellow Sage (on government seal of Southern St. Martin) Coralita
NATIONAL TREE:	Flamboyant (also called Poinciana and "July Tree")
NATIONAL BIRD:	Brown Pelican
PATRIOTIC AND POPULAR SONGS:	"Emancipation Song" (This traditional song is also called the "Brim" song. "Brim" is the refrain sound of the Emancipation song while it is sung to movements of the Ponum) "O Sweet St. Martin Land" (by Ft. Gerard Kemps) "St. Martin is My Home" (by Lino Hughes & The Hardways) "St. Martin is Nice" (by Tounka and Friends) "Sweet Little St. Martin" (by Ramon Wilson and Spencer Jeffers)
NATIONAL DANCE:	Ponum (also pronounced Panam)
NATIONAL DAYS/ FESTIVALS:	Mardi Gras, begins February in Marigot Treaty of Concordia Day, March 23 (signed in 1648) Easter Monday/Family Day (Monday following Easter Sunday in April) St. Martin Carnival, mid-April to early May in Great Bay (Philipsburg) Emancipation Day, May 27 (official holiday in St. Martin-North) Emancipation Day, July 1 (St. Martin-South) St. Martin Thanksgiving Day (First Sunday in November, marks ending of Atlantic hurricane season)[4] St. Martin Day, November 11

[4]*Formerly held as a church service in September (Autumnal Equinox - "When the sun crossed the line.")*

NATIONAL MONUMENTS AND RESERVES:	Frontier Monument • Fort St. Louis (Marigot Fort) Fort Amsterdam • Ancestral Graves (Bishop Hill "Slave" Cemetery) Frontier Rock Wall (along the Union Road and running along the "partition" line of the island. Rock Walls, which can be seen along many roadways, are also known as "slave walls" as many were built hundreds of years ago by our enslaved ancestors to separate the various plantations or estates) • Bellevue Sugarmill Ruins Foga Salt Ruins • Moho Petroglyph • The Court House Paradise Peak • Water Spring (Colombier) Union/Bellevue Road • Public Well (Marigot) • Great Salt Pond Simpson Bay Lagoon • Baie de l'Embouchure (Coconut Grove) Belvedere National Park
NATIONAL DISHES:	Fish and Fungi • Stewed Goat, Rice and Pigeon Peas Saltfish, Dumplings, and Provisions • Green Banana and Fish • St. Martin-style Chicken Lokrio (also pronounced Lokri) • Conchs and Dumplings • (Stewed green pigeon peas is a popular side dish. Chicken Leg and Johnny Cake is a popular snack or "fast food.")
NATIONAL DRINK:	Guavaberry (liqueur)
POPULAR SOUPS:	Callaloo Soup • Pigeon Peas Soup and Dumplings
POPULAR DRINKS AND LIQUEURS:	Mauby • Soursop Juice • Tamarind Juice • Sorrel Juice Lime Punch (a liqueur) • Lime Juice (St. Martin style) Shodo (an egg-nog drink) • Prickly Pear Liqueur Beauperthuy Punch

POPULAR DESSERTS AND TRADITIONAL SWEETS:	Coconut Tart • Sweet Potato Pudding • Black Cake Pound Cake • Sookdice • Banana Fritters • Pumpkin Fritters • Sugarcakes (coconut) • Peanut Sugarcakes Five-fingers • Sugardaddy • Peppermint Candy
TRADITIONAL JELLIES, JAMS, AND PRESERVES:	Guava Jelly • Guavaberry Jam • Stewed Tamarind (preserve) Gooseberry (preserve) • Wild Cherry (preserve) "Cherrynut" (preserve)
POPULAR AND TRADITIONAL BREADS:	In addition to regular brick-oven and modern oven-baked bread and "bakes," cassava bread, "leaven dough" bread and corn cake were popular traditional breads up to the 1960s. The rich-tasting, non-greasy St. Martin Johnny Cake remains a popular home-made and commercial bread.
POPULAR FRUITS:	Sugarapple • Mammy • Kinnip (also spelled genip) • Mango Cherrynut • Gooseberry • Pommeserette • Soursop Mesapple • Custard Apple • Sea Grape • Hog Plum Sugar Plum • Plum • Locust ("Stinking Toe") • Banana, Fig Blogo (Hog Banana) • Almond • Tamarind • Papaya "Cherries"

The creative word

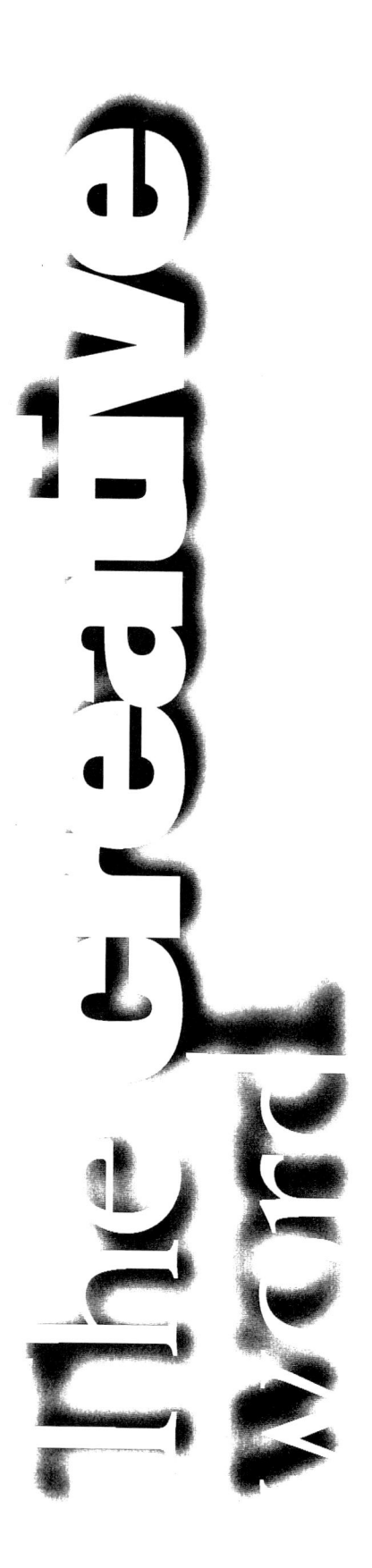

The "sayings" or proverbs of Traditional St. Martin are not just verbal artifacts of an old cultural legacy or oral records of the common folk and their old-time way of life. More than for their age-old value, proverbs like the few gathered here, are ageless, living testimonies of the people's creative and adaptive genius.

The proverbs known as "native" to Sweet St. Martin reflect the "memory" of pragmatism and wisdom from older cultures and civilizations—especially of the African but also of the European. Some are unique to the St. Martin Experience. Some are known throughout the Caribbean, worded differently perhaps, and thus wed common ancient origins and insular uniqueness to the centuries' old integration process, and out of which is evolving a sovereign Caribbean civilization. Some are of a wider New World creation, and others are by now the preserve of all humanity and their origins obscure.

The St. Martin "sayings," from the bawdy to the sublime, constitute a profound intellectual activity by a people whose reflection on life was by the sweat of their brow. The St. Martin folk, thus, began to define their immediate reality and claim a rightful place in the world a long time ago. The folk "sayings" or proverbs are then the creative encoding of the people's knowledge and capacity to coexist, change, and transform natural and societal environments and "overstand" the necessary symbiotic relationships. The "sayings" are at the root of a national "language" and are elemental to the continuing formation of a philosophy, a way of life, and a world view—a St. Martin identity that is creative and dynamic.

According to Dr. Jan Knappert: "The purpose of proverbs is not a fixed function in every recurrent identical situation. Proverbs are flexible parts of human understanding in this world, ready to be adapted and applied to suit a particular, unique situation. Like people, proverbs have to function in an ever-changing unpredictable world, or be lost. ... Proverbs are made not only for learning, but for pleasure too, and often for a refreshing laugh."

The following short list of "sayings" or proverbs, some of which influenced and even directed the daily life of the Survivalist Period (1648-1848) and Traditional St. Martin (1848-1963), were compiled mostly by Wilfred Roumou. Many of the proverbs were introduced into conversation by first saying "Meh choil," or "Meh dear."

All grin teeth t'ain' laugh.

Old fire sticks burn quick.

Still mouth keeps wise head.

What goes up comes down.

Never spit in the sky; it will fall in your face.

Still water runs deep.

Barking dogs seldom bite.

Massa cow, massa bull.

Never get between the tree and its bark.

Roaches have no business in fowl's nest.

Never burn the bridge you pass over.

Never cut down the tree that gives you shade.

Monkey knows what tree to jump on.

Don't be a carry-go-bring-come.

Tell the truth and you never have to remember not to forget.

Never hang your hat higher than you can reach.

Look before you leap.

Very-well will tell Not-so-well "Hold on a little longer."

While the grass is growing the horse is starving.

A stitch in time saves nine.

Never count your chickens before the eggs hatch.

Never put all your eggs in one basket.

You will never see fowl's behind until wind blows.

Let-alone better than Beg-pardon.

What sweetens goat's mouth sours his behind.

Talk is cheap; tobacco costs money.

Distance makes the heart grow fonder.

Nothing comes from an empty coal bag but dust.

Empty bag can't stand up.

What hurts eyes makes nose run.

Blood is thicker than water.

Long run for meager goat.

Hungry dog eats raw corn.

Make haste, less speed.

Birds of a feather flock together.

Where horse reach, jackass will reach also.

Cattle-boy knows cattle's temper.

Pure water comes from the head of the fountain.

To beat dog find a stick.

Bald head men never part with their combs.

Tall trees catch much wind.

Every dog has his day, and every hog his Saturday.

Moonlight may run; daylight will sure catch her.

Do your best and God will the rest.

Every day bucket goes to the well, one of these days the rope will burst.

Please, I'm no bamboo to cover the rain.

He who has the watch must keep the look-out.

Who has quaw-quaw in the sun must keep eye for rain.

Small boat carries big sail.

Time is money.

If you care, you will share.

Never ask how much but ask how good.

Where there is smoke, there is fire.

The darkest hour is just before dawn.

Behind every dark cloud is a silver lining.

Old broom sweeps cleaner than new broom.

Never be wrong and strong.

What you have bought you will have to wear.

You can run but you can't hide.

What soberness would have concealed drunkenness has revealed.

When Jack says "Walk," Tom, you better run.

If you sleep with dogs, you must catch fleas.

Who don't hear does feel.

Mangoes don't fall far from the tree.

He who lives in glass house shouldn't throw stones.

What you sow you reap.

He who laughs last laughs best.

When monkey can't reach the grapes he says they are sour.

Love-so don't have-so.

Meh dear, if barracuda comes out of the sea and tell you sprat does poison you will have to believe him.

One rotten mango spoils the bunch.

Never put a monkey to watch bananas.

Who has butter on his head must keep out of the sun.

Honesty is the best policy.

Don't put the cart in front of the horse.

What goes around comes around.

Today for me, tomorrow for you.

My Lord God is high, but he sees below.

Once burned, twice shy.

Actions speak louder than words.

Silence gives consent.

To trust someone you must have confidence in him.

What is joke for the butcher is death for the hog.

Your own lice will bite the hardest.

Soon ripe, soon rot.

Monkey says what he has in his jaw-bone is his own.

One bird in your hand is worth one hundred in the bushes.

Don't give me a cock-and-bull story; later you will tell me guinea-cock brings guinea-hen.

Make sure your brains are engaged before you put your mouth in motion.

Have pride in your work, and your work will support you.

A man's word should be so great that he should be able to stake his life on it.

When you have bad luck, wet paper will cut you.

Your own is your own, even if you have it in a spoon.

If someone doesn't like you, they will give you a basket to carry water.

While your brother's beard is burning, soak yours.

You never miss the water till the well runs dry.

When town is asleep, thief is on the prowl.

Don't be like the cow that gave a good pail of milk, and then kicked it over.

I can't wrangle; you have the handle, I have the blade.

When filth stinks, it doesn't care who it dabs.

A dirty hog will brush against the king.

Be careful with those who are quick to promise; they are nearly always late to deliver.

When rum in, wits out.

Don't get fried in your own fat.

Meh choil, lingeh-longah spells Dutch, but your manners desire much.

Never trouble Trouble unless Trouble troubles you.

When you can tell Back wait, you can't tell Belly wait.

In a pasture where cattle fight, no grass grows.

If a man can't return your stare, he has something to fear.

Dog needs his tail to fan fly from his behind just one more time.

You must look for black sheep before dark.

Two man-crab can't live in the same hole.

Spit your cough where you caught it.

Play fool to catch wise.

Copper plate etching: "Bridge at Grand Case (1977)," by Roland Richardson.

Chapter 2

FACES OF THE PEOPLE

Up from the bitter shackles of the past,
Up from the strangling yoke of Tyranny,
Through valleys green, through mountain ranges vast,
Thunders the strident voice of Liberty!

O Sweet St. Martin of a thousand dreams,
O golden goddess of the tropic seas,
Betrayed by despots in their greedy schemes,
Your honor stained—your glory on its knees

Arise! Arise and hear the clarion voice
Of Freedom shouting forth from shore to shore.
Let every patriot's fervent heart rejoice
And smash the chains of shame forever more!

—CHARLES BORROMEO HODGE,
Up From The Shackles

FORERUNNERS OF ST. MARTIN'S FREEDOM

Maroons and St. Martin

The Maroons of the Black Experience in the Caribbean and the Americas—from as early as 1503, but more so between 1518, when Charles V granted permission for four thousand Africans to be sent as slaves to the Antilles, to 1888, when Brazil became the last country in the hemisphere to abolish slavery—were the most militant and independent manifestations of the fight for freedom.

Maroons, often called runaways, were the Blacks who escaped from slavery and hid or lived in the forests, swamps, caves, secluded bays, keys, inhospitable mountains, and hills. In some instances, Maroons mingled—like the so-called "illegal immigrants" in the twentieth century Caribbean—with freed Africans in the "town." Historian Franklin Knight is illustrative to the point: "The long history of the Maroons in all the colonies bore eloquent testimony to the unquenchable will to be free that permeated every slave-holding society."

The Maroons of St. Martin pre-date the 1648 Treaty of Concordia. By January 6, 1734, the island's *marronage* activities forced authorities to pass another in a series of laws prescribing what to do with *"maronnegers."* These brave, freedom-loving Africans were to be shot in the foot if they resisted capture, stated the law. Those captured were returned to the "watch commander" so that the person or people who hunted and captured Maroons could be paid. In a statement posted in the late 1780s, again by authorities in Great Bay: "Run-away slaves that are caught and imprisoned and are not being released by their owners against payment of the costs incurred, can be auctioned after 6 weeks if the owner lives on the island, otherwise after 3 months." Similar laws were common in the island's North.

The Maroon phenomenon existed parallel to the slave system. However, *marronage* is only now becoming standard study in Caribbean schools and liberation literature. Though yet to be popularized in song, theater, movies, and children's literature, it represents a singularly glorious chapter of the spirit of Caribbean manhood and the very bedrock of Caribbean nationhood. Cuban scholars may have written most definitively about Maroon societies. These societies were called Palenques in some Spanish and English colonies and Quilombos in the Portuguese colony of Brazil. The Cubans inform us that the Maroon phenomenon was not homogenous in its manifestation. There were Maroon individuals, a family, or small groups of hunter-gatherer families who hid out in the forest, swamp, or cave. There were dreaded Maroon bands, mostly men, that raided plantations for weapons, goods, food, and women who were taken to their camps as mates. There were large self-sustaining Maroon communities and nations.

Maroon nations, led by powerful men and women such as Zimbi of Brazil, Nanny of Jamaica, and Joli-Coeur of Suriname, had a government, fed their citizens, defended their borders militarily, entered into peace treaties with "local" authorities, and exacted tributes from European governments. The most famous Maroon nations were located in the Blue Mountains and other precipitous peaks of Jamaica; in Palmeres, Brazil—legendary for its capoeira warriors who defeated Dutch and Portuguese expeditions; in the forest and along the rivers of Suriname; and in St. Vincent, where Maroons existed since 1667, some being escapees from neighboring Barbados. In St. Vincent, the Africans and Island Caribs—having been enemies and allies before becoming known as "Black Caribs"—were able to join forces against European invaders and oppressors. The Maroons and Caribs controlled the island for extensive periods. The Maroon Wars of Jamaica and Suriname, their rivalries and wars of defense, are well documented. (Descendants of Maroons in Jamaica and Suriname enjoy certain political autonomy and a distinct cultural identity to this day.) Led by notable chiefs such Osceola, whose wife was sold into slavery, Seminole Indians and Black runaways inter-married and constituted a virtual Maroon nation in Florida's everglades between 1818 and 1842.

The fragmented records of Maroon leaders, fortifications, and exploits against the colonial authorities and their better equipped armies in Dominica, Hispaniola, Ecuador, Mexico, and especially Panama, read like epics. In the Mavis C. Campbell study, between the 1540s and 1570s: "As the British were soon to complain in Jamaica that they feared the Maroons more than they did the Spaniards, so also was the complaint of the Spaniards at this time, fearing more the Blacks than the British."

The ranks of Maroons were constantly being swollen by runaways—including men, women, and children on the run following slave rebellions. Maroon activities helped slave revolts in many ways. The Haitian Revolution might not have triumphed were it not for the militarism, guerrilla tactics, hiding places, social organization, and communication network of the Maroons. In rare cases, conflicts between Maroons and the plantocracy simultaneously stretched the former to their defensible and sustainable limits, and pushed the latter to the verge of economic collapse because of raids and the increase in runaways. Consequently, the colonists conceded to stop their attacks and large Maroon societies, "tribes" (as they were called in Suriname), or nations, agreed to return fugitives to the plantation. This tactic often bought the tribe time to rebuild its defensive system after a war and later accommodate more refugees.

Individual and small-group Maroons were subject to a tense nomadic existence because of slave-catchers. The authorities and plantation owners rewarded slave-catchers for capturing runaways. When ordering anti-Maroon campaigns, the authorities encouraged soldiers and slave-catchers to rape and otherwise abuse women and children caught at Maroon encampments. A colonial council resolution in the late 1660s Jamaica stated: "... if any number of (*person*) shall find out the Pallenque of the said Negroes, they shall have and enjoy to their uses the Women and Children, and all the plunder they can find there for their reward." Campbell found out, "... so far as the whites were concerned, (*this*) was counterproductive because any abuse of Maroon women was invariably met with the most serious consequences to the perpetrators" from Maroon men. Colonists even offered "pardon from what is past" to a captured Maroon who would betray the secret location of his or her camp, and freedom to a slave and indentured white for "killing and takeing any of the said villaines."

The Maroons sometimes stood at a quarter or more of the African population in the colonies. In 1720 Venezuela, wrote ethnologist Miguel Acosta Saignes, *Cimarrónes*, as Maroons were called in Spanish, numbered about twenty thousand strong. At the beginning of the nineteenth century, as the *Cimarrónes* continued to spread throughout "la Provincia de Venezuela," the enslaved population stood at sixty thousand men, women, and children.

Maroons neither bought, begged for, nor were granted their freedom. They were the tens of thousands—among the millions of enslaved—who took their freedom. Maroons were proud and self-reliant. They governed their own communities, established lines of communication that were not dependent on the authority of the whites, and were a crucial internal factor in the eventual destruction of the slave system. Some Maroons were notoriously scornful of their plantation brethren. Plantation owners, slave-drivers, church and government officials in turn, fed the enslaved a steady dose of "news" about "wild savages, starving in the bush." As a result, to this day, in Suriname and elsewhere, when many Blacks refer to "the bush," too often it is done as a put-down and not hailed with manly pride as a freedom symbol.

According to St. Martin political scientist Joseph H. Lake, Jr., a most critical feature of *marronage* is that for over the three hundred and fifty years of slavery, tens of thousands of Africans in the hemisphere were "born here" free and lived out their lives as free men and women in Maroon societies. Campbell cited another generally overlooked position: "The Maroons in the New World were the first in this hemisphere to strike a blow for freedom—as far as recorded history goes. And it is in this sense that they can be seen as the first Americans."

St. Martin Maroon activities were related mostly to the individual and small subsistence group. (There was also absenteeism or *petite marronage*. This occurred when a slave left the plantation without permission, to visit a lover, child or other family member sold to another plantation; or to escape the immediate drudgery of slavery. After hiding out and conducting his or her visits at night, the man or woman would reappear days, weeks, or months later. The returning slave would be tortured.) St. Martin Maroons inhabited the forested hills, Maho Reef cave system, Lowlands, Anse Marcel area, or escaped to neighboring islands. They subsisted on fish, birds, provisions from their hidden "gardens," and crops and other goods from raided farms and plantations. St. Martin's Maroon heroine, One-Tété Lohkay, would raid the estates that ranged from "Industry" to what is today Saunders, St. Peters, Marigot Hill, and South Reward.

Great Bay passed an anti-Maroon law in 1796: "Because of the robberies committed at night ... slaves that are encountered on the streets after 9 o'clock at night without a note will for the attempt be publicly punished with the common negro punish-

St. Martin Maroons signaling to escape boat.

ment." On January 24, 1798, though the French Revolution had disrupted slavery on the island, in the South where the plantocracy and salt-pan owners were regaining their old power to enslave, a law was passed: "In order to avoid the fleeing of slaves, owners have to report their 'canoes, sail, pleasure and fishing boats,' that has to be furnished with a number. ..." After British invaders in 1801, and Napoleon in 1802, re-instituted slavery, a law was passed against the "sale of gunpowder and weapons to slaves."

In spite of oppressive laws designed to keep Blacks enslaved, "a good many" escaped across the sea to Anguilla, Trinidad, and other islands—probably more so after 1801, when slavery was re-established after the hiatus beginning in 1795, and certainly after the British Parliament passed the Emancipation Act in 1833. St. Martin also served as a Maroon haven. In one account, a runaway rowed a boat from St. Eustatius to St. Martin.

There are curious notes to the evolution and related uses of the word maroon. In Grenada the word referred to collective community building of a house or barn (Jollification in St. Martin). In olden St. Martin, Blacks and whites referred to a picnic far away from the plantation or one's house (i.e. to Pinel Key), as a maroon. Up to the 1960s, the lavish cock-fight fêtes in Northern St. Martin were called "maroons." In Northern Cul-de-sac, there is a tree referred to as "the maroon tree."

Maroons were the first authentic heroes, heroines, freedom fighters, and nation builders of today's Caribbean people. Their spirit of independence remains elemental to the attainment of Caribbean sovereignty. Their legacy is evident in the independent *raison d'être* of the Haitian and Cuban revolutions; in the historical origins and redemption outlook of RasTafari; in the *Grito de Lares* rebellion in Puerto Rico and the aborted Grenadian Revolution; in the Marcus Garvey[5] movement which is at the root of the resilient search for genuine independence by Caribbean "territories" and countries; in the heart and purpose of those who voted for independence in the "St. Maarten Referendum" of October 14, 1994; in every act of resistance against colonialism, imperialism, racism, and oppressive "local" rulers; and in every instance of love and labor that claims the Caribbean by and for its people in the ongoing engagement to build free, independent, democratic, creative, just, and prosperous societies.

[5] *Marcus Garvey was a direct descendant of Jamaica's Maroons.*

The Revolt and Massacre of 1830

On September 26, 1830, Blacks of St. Martin made a heroic bid for their freedom. According to St. Martin diarist Joseph Emmanuel Richardson (1874-1949), "The Proclamation of Louis Philippe as King of France is made in Marigot, and the red, white, blue flag is hoisted" on the fated date. "At this moment, the slaves believed that they would be free, and because of this deception, many were killed. ..."

The Blacks who rallied to freedom stood their ground when ordered back to the plantation. Freed Blacks in the small town of Marigot, and possibly Maroons, very likely participated in the manifestation. The revolt is met with the armed might of plantation owners, colonial officials, and soldiers. Many Blacks of St. Martin were massacred.

How many martyrs fell for freedom that day? What were their names? That is not yet known to us. The bloodletting was not in vain, however. Memories of the island-wide easing of the slave whip between 1795 and 1801, and the inextinguishable dream of freedom, pushed a number of our courageous ancestors to seek refuge in the hills, bays, and other hiding places. Later, with the cry of freedom and the smell of their unarmed kin's blood still in the air and in their consciousness, "A good few," wrote Richardson, "were able to escape to Anguilla. From there, they went to Trinidad in order to enjoy the freedom that was accorded to the English slaves." While *marronage* has been dated to January 6, 1734, it is not clear if Richardson's "escape" occurred in 1830, after the rebellion, or after the British Parliament's Emancipation Act of 1833. The Emancipation Act of 1833 abolished slavery in Britain's Caribbean colonies and initiated an apprenticeship system. The English abolition was implemented in July of 1834.

What about the "deception" which made the ancestors believe they "would be released from bondage" in 1830? That was due in part to the news and views of the day. There was a general perception in the colonies, and in France, that Louis Philippe would establish the second revolution by instituting profound democratic changes. The outbreak of the French (1788) and the Haitian (1791) revolutions had forever changed perceptions and possibilities about the "Rights of Man" and national independence in the colonies. To educator and historian Daniella Jeffry, Philippe was a bourgeois type and did sympathize with democratic ideas that grew out of 1789, when the French Revolution first triumphed. Supporters of the July Revolution of 1830 "would take hold of anyone to lead the democratic cause." Philippe, who joined the national guard during the revolt, appeared ready and able.

In *The Caribbean – The Genesis of a Fragmented Nationalism*, historian Franklyn W. Knight stated that, "The second revolution of 1830 created elected councils in Martinique and Guadeloupe from a rather limited electorate." As a dependency of Guadeloupe, the North of St. Martin experienced this increased "representation" in local government for eligible members of the plantocracy. Jeffry noted, however, that King Louis Philippe refused to further reform the electoral system. This helped to make him unpopular with the left and right until the end of his reign with the February Revolution of 1848. Known as the "bourgeois king" or "'citizen king' because of his bourgeois manner and dress," King Philippe accumulated a great fortune for himself while on the throne, through private speculation and banking. He was chased from office by "the mob"—called out again, this time by near bankrupt bankers and businessmen. It should be remembered that in 1793, Philippe had deserted the French Revolution army. The monarch also had little to do, if anything, with the abolition of slavery in the Antilles, though slavery was abolished in France in 1836.

When Richardson retired from the civil service in 1947, he had served as secretary of the Mairie in Marigot, harbor master, court translator, and land surveyor. He was also a life-long farmer. The diarist often recounted for his family in Rambaud a history of St. Martin that was a personal and yet profound graft of the Oral Tradition. Richardson's writings were compounded by records he had access to as a learned man and high-ranking civil servant. One of his entries dispelled the paternalistic and emasculating notion that slavery in St. Martin was wholly less severe than anywhere else in the hemisphere, that masters were benevolent, and slaves were happy and not rebellious. After signing the Treaty of Concordia in 1648, wrote Richardson, the North or "French" part of the island "is divided into four sections: ... Marigot, Colombier,

Grand Case, and Orleans. Each plantation owns a certain number of slaves and the animals needed for the cultivation and transport of the sugarcane.

"You can hear all day long the cracking of the whip on recalcitrant backs, the sound of the hoe and the cries and the crying of those poor unfortunate slaves, obliged to submit to this hateful yoke." And again we see how culture nourished the humanity and perseverance of the ancestors during those ghastly pale centennial hours of our early history in the Caribbean: "But sometimes on moonlit nights, the poor slaves would dance their Ouatouba, their Bamboulley. Then they would sing the songs of their country.

"Sometimes they cry after listening to the traditional songs of their homeland."

Richardson's "History of St. Martin" is hardly exhaustive. It is an honest statement, a reflection, and, as he was able to ascertain, it recorded "the state of affairs." Richardson's diary is essentially the native's search for his and her people's role in history and the struggle to establish social, cultural, political, and economic freedom. Through this search, are also unearthed the realities of a people striving invariably for independence, justice, peace, democracy, and prosperity in a land they must totally claim as their own. A more conscious search fuels the evolution of a new perspective of history. Hidden and new victories are claimed, truths long crushed to the ground rise in full bloom, martyrs made known, and every blow struck for freedom sanctioned.

The fruits of a more conscious search will serve as inspiration for every child of St. Martin to commit faithfully to building a just, united, independent, democratic, and progressive Caribbean nation. This is a people's living history, told for the love of St. Martin, not an acquiescence for the glory of planters and salt-pan owners of an unjust and brutal slave system. Unlike Monsieur Martin, the nostalgic French commander of the island's North in 1866, at the demise of slavery we do not mourn or yearn for "... Those splendid plantations of which, alas, there remains no more than a shadow and sad memory."

One-Tété Lohkay
b.? – d.?

There once was a woman enslaved on a plantation in St. Martin. Her name was Lohkay. She was a proud and brave woman. She defied the beastly evils of slave masters, overseers, and the injustices of the plantation.

The memory of this Maroon heroine has been protected from oblivion in the bosom of oral history and legend. Over a century after striking out for freedom, Lohkay emerges as a phoenix, serving St. Martin's national and human destiny.

Rebellious Black women on Caribbean slave plantations were called "spitfires." In Lucille Mathurin's pioneer research of colonial records, rebel women are referred to as "evil," "lazy," "violent," "insolent," and "incorrigible." Their punishment for "talking back," refusing to work like beasts of burden, or running away was the same as the punishment dished out to enslaved men. For fighting slave-drivers and other aggressive acts against the barbarism of the European slave system, Black women were labeled as having an "Amazonian cast of character." The punishment for defying slavery, from Barbados to Martinique, from St. Martin to The Bahamas, from Cuba to Tobago (and throughout the Americas), included flogging, being sold to another plantation or off the island, body dismemberment, imprisonment for life, and death.

Enslaved women commanded what one commandant in colonial Trinidad called, "that powerful instrument of attack and defence, their tongue." Mathurin added, "that numerous slave women in fact, showed little fear of their superiors, and did not hesitate to answer back." Spitfires were at the cutting edge of a tradition of personal defiance, work slow-downs, and sabotage. They led their sisters and children in joining with their men to plan and execute plantation burnings, revolts, and escape from bondage.

Lohkay was a spitfire in the South of St. Martin. Her stand for human dignity made the life of drudgery intolerable. This drove her to seek freedom by running away. Lohkay was hunted down, recaptured, and returned to the plantation. She was beaten severely. The authorities ordered that one of her breasts be cut off. She became known as One-Tété Lohkay.

Cutting off the breasts of Black women who ran away or were involved in uprisings was not uncommon while the unholy institution reigned in the Caribbean and Americas. Another punishment for rebel women was "the pit." In the writings of St. Martin's Carlos Cooks: "This mode of torture was reserved for pregnant Black women. It consisted of a hole in the ground, deep enough to house her belly, with her naked back exposed to the slave master's bull whip. If her condition of pregnancy was in advanced state and her offence against the slave system was a serious one, she would be whipped until she prematurely gave birth to the child in the womb, or died from the excruciating pain of the bull whip into her naked flesh."

The crime against Lohkay went unpunished, as did the criminals. Laws protected the plantation, government, church, military, and other white figures that raped, mutilated, crippled, and otherwise abused and exploited Black human bodies. One law in Great Bay authorized slave-catchers, usually Dutch and French soldiers or poor whites of different nationalities, to shoot the fugitive in the foot if the "slave" resisted recapture. Slaves were thought of and treated as the slave master's property. Therefore, murdering a rebellious slave was not as frequent as torture, mutilation, and imprisonment.

Lohkay was tended by the plantation's "bush doctor," using the herbal medicines of St. Martin. Lohkay rose from her sick-bed, uncowered and even more determined to be free. She was warned that if her insolence persisted the other breast would be ripped off her body. In *The Rebel Woman in The British West Indies During Slavery*, "... punishments got increasingly severe with each repeated offence. ..." A slave threatened with punishment might also "try to escape before the threat was carried out."

One-Tété Lohkay ran away again! Not only did the brave rebel remain free, but according to Oral Tradition, she regularly raided the plantations in Southern Cul-de-sac for foodstuff and goods, and no doubt to visit with her people.

Photographer and student of St. Martin's proverbs, Wilfred Roumou, recalled the admiration with which his grandmother referred to One-Tété Lohkay: how she lived freely in the hills; how at times her temporary camp-fire could be seen at night from the plantation mansions and shacks below. At dawn, as the enslaved were being herded out to field, smoke from Lohkay's night camp could be seen spiraling up to the heavens. Thus she became a living legend.

The name of One-Tété Lohkay is to be heralded by all St. Martiners and freedom-loving people. Hers is a kindred spirit to Nanny of Jamaica, Queen Mary and Bottom Belly of the Virgin Islands, Harriet Tubman of the USA, and other champions of freedom who burst the chains of slavery and dealt mortal blows to the plantation and its rulers.

St. Martin's Emancipation of 1848

Emancipation from the unholy institution of slavery came to the Blacks of the entire island of St. Martin in 1848. Before this time, the Europeans wrote of "the inhabitants" of "the colony" of St. Martin and "the slaves." "Slaves" to the European "inhabitants" in the Caribbean and Americas were not people but property.

However, the struggle for human dignity, freedom, justice, and advancement, permeated the lives of the enslaved and free Africans or Blacks in St. Martin, and throughout the hemisphere. This constant mental, moral, and material struggle countered the dehumanization wrought by slavery. Maroons or runaways; establishing Maroon nations such as in St. Vincent, Jamaica, Suriname, and Brazil; sabotage of plantation equipment; burning of plantation mansions and crops; a history replete with courageous rebellions; and the Haitian Revolution, were significant features of the war against the European slave system by Black individuals and groups—from the beginning of slavery in the early sixteenth century to its inglorious demise in the late nineteenth century.

The enslaved, freedmen, and Maroons played the most active role in their own liberation. This impacted on and compounded the wider economic, political, and social conditions that militated against the perpetuation of the slave trade and plantation economy lorded over by the white population's ruling class. The region's European population, pointed out historian Franklin Knight, "dominated the administrative machinery of local government, the militia, and the established churches." What constituted the social force of the struggle for human dignity and freedom? The ways in which the Black ancestors were able to maintain, transform, or syncretize cultures of the various African tribes, states, and kingdoms of origin. The ancestors forged new and splendidly dynamic cultural forms out of their mostly hostile New World experience and environment.

In the late 1700s, explained Knight, the white rulers in the Caribbean who "... had never considered the colonies their home," began to feel the internal tensions, political pressures from the metropolis, and changing conditions of world trade which forced them to accept ... amelioration of the conditions of slavery as a compromise position between the status quo and the total abolition of the barbarous system. That failed—as did the international sugar market to which they felt irrevocably tied."

In St. Martin, slavery was first discontinued in 1795, when French republicans, still fueled by the historic French Revolution of 1789, captured the whole island and sequestered plantations. The Blacks, especially in the North, became free land-tillers under a supervisor called a *sequestre*. Around 1798, the "Dutch side" plantocracy and salt-pan owners, ruling in Great Bay with a sort of permission from the French, began to regain their power to enact legislation in favor of the slave system.

In 1801, Blacks, without political, economic, educational, and military organization and power to maintain and advance their freedom as a group, were thrown back into slavery by the British who invaded and controlled St. Martin until 1802.

Napoleon Bonaparte re-instituted slavery in the French colonies in 1802. Guadeloupe's "Magnanimous warrior," Louis Delgrés, led an armed revolt against the enemy expeditions sent from France. On May 28, that same year, he was killed. His poorly armed rebels, their women and children were slaughtered at Matouba. Napoleon decided to re-conquer Saint-Domingue, failed miserably at the hands of the Haitian revolutionaries, but managed to kidnap the liberator Toussaint L'ouverture (Haiti was declared independent by the great Jean-Jacques Dessalines in 1804).

In St. Martin, a law passed in Great Bay in 1786, could still be evoked to force freed Blacks to wear a red ribbon pinned to their chests. The enslaved had to wear a "visible" badge identifying the slave master who sent the slave on errands between quarters, plantations, and from one side of the island to the next. Failure to carry the slave badge resulted in a monetary fine for the slave master and a severe whipping for the slave. (Variations of this law were enacted and enforced throughout the Caribbean. Failure to show the badge or pass to any white person who asked for it, gave the white person authority to flog the slave.) Other laws called for beatings and imprisonment for Blacks who bought on credit, loaned each other money, sold salt from the Great Salt Pond, farmed their own "gardens" on the edge of plantations, and had dance parties after eight o'clock at night. One law commanded

Blacks to greet every white person they came in contact with.

Between 1813 and 1818, Holland and Sweden abolished the slave trade. France declared the slave trade illegal in 1818. Spain followed suit in 1820—on receipt of £400,000. The rulings did not end the smuggling of slaves into and out of St. Martin.

Caribbean scholar Dr. A. F. Paula claimed that slavery in St. Martin between 1816 and 1848 "did not exhibit the characteristic harsh treatment of slaves of the time ... and ... could be attributed to the declining economic conditions at the beginning of the nineteenth century. ... This meant that masters and slaves had to co-operate more closely in order to survive." Dr. Paula's assertion should not lend itself to the notion held by some that slaves in St. Martin were treated better than elsewhere, and that "good masters" took care of their slaves while a wholly obedient slave community worked hard for the masters. The inventory of crimes against humanity during slavery and imperial domination in St. Martin and throughout the hemisphere, vigorously contradicts this notion. The laws passed by insular authorities and other records of the day prove the notion of a master/slave paradise in St. Martin to be a false and horrible distortion of historic facts. Dr. Paula noted too the evidence of insubordination, growing freedom consciousness, and "independent attitude" among slaves in St. Martin. He connected these mainly to "... the British emancipation of slaves in 1833," and "... the economy of the island, especially the economic activity surrounding the gathering of salt. ...

"In contrast of this, the sugar plantations on the island were not popular amongst the slaves. ... Dutch slaves were thus accustomed to working with free labourers and slaves from French St. Martin and free labourers from the surrounding islands. This made them feel as though they were in some sense free themselves." Socialization in the Great Salt Pond and salt-pans of Grand Case, Orleans, Chevrise, and Red Pond forged a solidarity between the enslaved and freed Africans and fueled the natural desire and informed drive for freedom.

On September 26, 1830, Blacks demonstrated for freedom in Marigot and were massacred by French authorities. The British Emancipation Act of 1833 was enforced in July of 1834. From 1833 to 1848, a "freedom canal" was opened by our courageous ancestors at the northwestern shores of St. Martin. To signal runaways and Maroons when it was time to escape, and to guide freedom-bound vessels across the Anguilla channel at night, flambeau codes were developed. Mindful of the sabotage of freedom in 1801, the revolt and massacre of 1830, and after the week-long 1848 emancipation celebration, elders warned their young against staying on the island. In his historical diary, Joseph E. Richardson wrote that many Blacks plunged the ocean for Trinidad—mulattoes sailed to St. Croix. Others went to Puerto Rico. They were propelled, like the boat people of the modern Caribbean, by the desire for a better life and thoughts that the unholy institution of slavery could return.

The Society for the Abolition of Slavery was founded in France by abolitionists in 1834. In 1836, slavery was declared illegal in France. In 1838, the British Emancipation Act was "finally" enforced throughout Britain's colonies in the Caribbean. In 1841, some French planters, possibly influenced by abolitionist François Auguste Perrinon and certainly by internal, regional, and international pressures, requested France to abolish slavery in the Northern part of St. Martin.

On May 27, 1848, the French government abolished slavery in its Caribbean colonies (Denmark also abolished slavery in its Caribbean colonies in 1848). Emancipation was not enforced in the French-controlled North of St. Martin until July of that year. The Blacks made up the "Brim" song: "Ah be been a hearum buh massa been a hidum (We have been hearing about it but master has been hiding it)." The song recorded the feeling and knowledge among Blacks that slave masters and other authorities lied and hid the news of emancipation. In *Making of an Island*, Jean Glasscock speculated that the news was hidden for economic reasons, "... since it occurred in the middle of the cane harvest. ..." This would have been nothing new. "In almost every colony the slaves felt that the local whites were deliberately obstructing the course of emancipation, which they were. They also felt," continued Knight, "especially when the agitation for complete abolition became intense after the 1830's, that they had already gotten their freedom, which they had not."

Emancipation news reached the South. Scores of slaves pelted across the Frontier to freedom and to look for work. Diamond Estate in Cole Cole Bay and "Freedom Path" on the Belvedere Estate were some of the escape routes North. According to writer S. J. Kruythoff, they "formed an alliance with their French brethren." Josiah Charles Waymouth wrote of "slaves" cowering in a Cole Bay Methodist church as if that image was typical

St. Martiners in the South, standing firm and united against slavery in 1848.

of St. Martin's Blacks, afraid to leave the plantation and claim their freedom. Some twentieth century historians and tourism writers seem to prefer this docile image—stubbornly maintaining that in 1848, "the slaves on the Dutchside preferred" to stay in bondage with their masters until 1863. However, other written records and oral traditions present the dominant image of a braver, bolder people who took that independent step on the road to freedom.

D. C. van Romondt wrote his interpretation in the following dramatic passage about the historic period of transition in which our ancestors stood their ground: "For this purpose (pillage and firing of plantations) they congregated on all the principal highways. Humanity shuddered at what might have been the possible result to all interested, had not the proprietors by an amelioration of the Penal Code calmed their excitement, to which effect, a process-verbal was made and signed by the principal proprietors in which they agreed to the people as if they were free. ..."

Notwithstanding the ensuing legal wrangling between planters and the Dutch Crown, persisting injustices, the struggle for better wages throughout the island, and the exodus of a number of the newly emancipated to Trinidad, St. Croix, Puerto Rico, and other islands, for all intents and purposes slavery in St. Martin, North and South, came to a whimpering end in 1848.

To Blacks, "Although Dutch and French St. Martin were divided politically and were autonomous in this regard, on the social level they formed a united slave community," wrote Dr. Paula in his pioneer study, *"Vrije" Slaven*.

In 1848, for the first time since post-Columbian settlement, the majority of this community marched into freedom, into the future, "united" as St. Martiners.

Diamond Estate 26

"Diamond Estate 26" refers to the entire population of twenty-six enslaved men, women, and children from the Diamond Estate or plantation in Cole Bay.

The Diamond Estate 26 planned and executed a successful escape from slavery after news of the May 27, 1848 emancipation in France's Caribbean colonies reached St. Martin. Our freedom-loving ancestors crossed the Frontier rock wall, built by slave labor. They entered the French-controlled North where slavery

The Diamond Estate 26 going North to freedom in 1848.

had been officially abolished. There they sought work and a better life. The Diamond Estate 26 were among the first people in the South to strike out for freedom after the deliberately hidden emancipation news reached the island's enslaved population. Writer Camille Baly has asserted that the news was kept from the enslaved by the plantocracy, salt-pan owners, government, and church officials until July, 1848. Jean Glasscock, in *Making of an Island*, suggested that the abolition was delayed "... to aid the planters ... since it occurred in the middle of the cane harvest."

News of emancipation spread throughout the island like wildfire. In the North, the emancipated made up the "Brim" or "Emancipation Song," beat the pump drum, and danced the Ponum around the "July Tree" (Flamboyant). This is why the Flamboyant, in fiery bloom at the time of emancipation, is St. Martin's National Tree. (Its branches were picked and waved in jubilation in 1848, just like the Haitians in St. Martin did in 1990, when news of Jean Bertrand Aristide's presidential election landslide swept through the Caribbean). In the South, our still officially enslaved ancestors committed acts of "economic" sabotage, went on "a general strike," and started running away. One group of escapees was cheered by kindred as its members requisitioned a boat anchored in Great Bay Harbor and made off into the distance.

Lieutenant Governor Johannes Willem van Romondt sent to Curaçao for additional Dutch soldiers to suppress the out-break of freedom. By the time the armed forces would have docked in Great Bay Harbor many days later, the labor situation would be changed. The people had changed forever. The plantocracy and salt-pan owners in the Dutch-controlled South were consequently forced by the people's actions to sign a procès-verbal, abandoning slavery immediately after emancipation was enforced in Northern St. Martin. The Dutch Kingdom abolished slavery in its other Caribbean colonies on July 1, 1863.

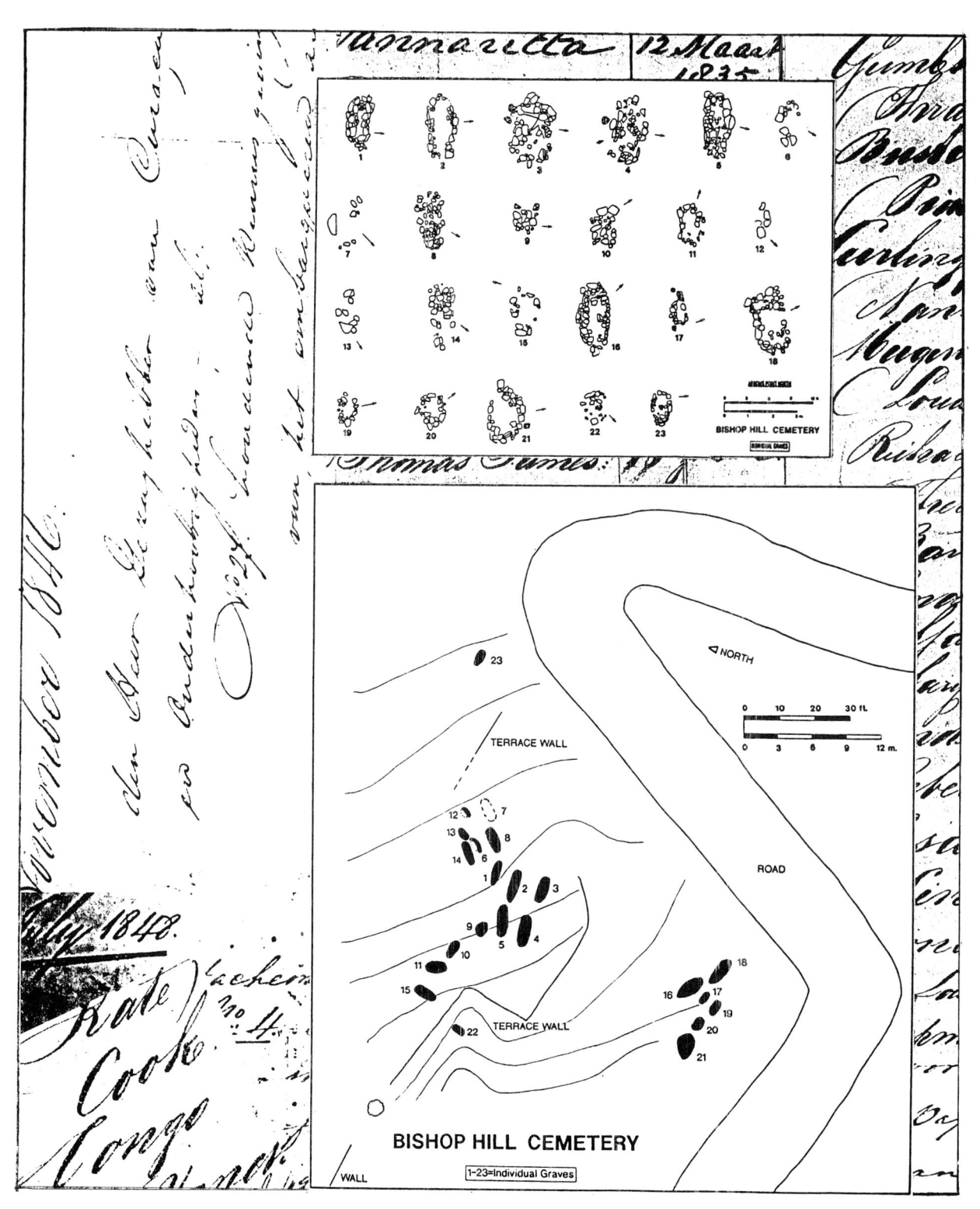

Graves of enslaved ancestors. Source: STINAPA-Sint Maarten, May 1993.

PROFILES OF
ST. MARTINERS IN HISTORY

Inez Eliza Baly-Lewis was a traditional midwife and masseuse who served St. Martin and occasionally the neighboring island of Anguilla. For a time, she was the traditional administrator of "the formula for the dead." The formula kept the human corpse from decomposing during the "nine-night" and other "wake" ceremonies that were usually held at the home of the deceased's family. Affectionately known throughout St. Martin as "Tan'tan Nez" or "Miss Nez," Baly-Lewis mothered twelve children and was well-versed in the nation's folklore and genealogy.

Miss Nez is best remembered, however, as an esteemed cultural worker. In 1982, Baly-Lewis revived the Ponum dance at the St. Maarten Festival of Arts & Culture (SMAFESTAC). The folk dancer, while up in age, thrilled the festival's audience with a memorable performance of the vivacious and graceful Ponum.

The Ponum Dance is thought to have evolved out of St. Martin's harvest/fertility rites and "popular" celebrations before 1848. The dance has retained African elements and it is today identified primarily with emancipation because it was danced openly in 1848, to celebrate the end of slavery.

The Ponum is St. Martin's National Dance because: *1.* Its historical value. *2.* Spiritual significance. *3.* Popularity throughout St. Martin's Survivalist (1648-1848) and Traditional (1848-1963) periods. *4.* Cultural originality and elegance.

The Ponum, often pronounced "Panam," and also known as the Pump Dance (because of the pump drum played), was danced regularly at fêtes well into the first half of the 1900s. Tan'tan Nez is considered the twentieth century's greatest Ponum dancer. She was a native of the hamlet of Freetown in St. Louis. St. Louis, Rambaud, and Colombier formed a vibrant cultural confederation of villages for much of Traditional St. Martin.

Tan'tan Nez was honored in 1988, by St. Maarten Council on the Arts through the efforts of dancer Carolyn Jenkins with a Certificate of Appreciation for her contribution to St. Martin dance.

1892-1939

"*Anthony Reynier Waters-Grovenhorst-Brouwer*[6] (born 1892 on Saba, died 1939 on St. Maarten) was a lawyer and an outspoken journalist on St. Maarten. He was the son of Abraham Jan Cornelius Brouwer and Marie Henrietta Waters-Grovenhorst. A. J. C. Brouwer was Lt. Governor of each of the Windward Islands (Saba, St. Eustatius, and St. Maarten) for a combined period of thirty years (1888-1918). It was during his term on Saba that his fifth and last child, A. R. W. G. Brouwer, was born. As the youngest child, he was called 'Broetje' by the family, later 'Broechie' by all those in St. Maarten who knew him.

"As his son, Engineer A. J. C. Brouwer who resides in Aruba tells us, 'Owing to the measly salary that my grandfather the Governor made in those days, the finances could not stretch for Broechie to go overseas to study, so he studied by correspondence and acquired two degrees, "Surveyor of Land" (*Landmeter*) and "Attorney-at-Law." However, since these degrees were from the U. S., his admeasurements were not recognized officially, and he was only allowed to appear in court as "Practitioner-of-Law" (*Practizijn*).' The 'new road' was surveyed and construction supervised by him. This road was later given the name A. J. C. Brouwersweg. Governor J. J. (Japa) Beaujon had this road named after Governor Brouwer because he read in the old archives how, for years, Governor Brouwer had fought and pleaded with Curacao for funds to build this road and finally succeeded.

"As a young man, 'Broechie' worked for a while as temporary assistant at the office of the Receiver-Postmaster of St. Maarten. He was honorably discharged upon his request on September 26th, 1910, owing to the fact that the Curacao 'bosses' wanted to transfer him to Curacao without a raise in salary.

"On December 22nd, 1934, he issued the first *De Slag om Slag (Blow for Blow)*, a weekly newspaper, in which he did not hesitate to criticize any corruption which took place in government. This newspaper appeared every Saturday morning and was printed at Mr. Brouwer's home on Front Street No. 61. ...

"Following in the footsteps of J. C. Waymouth and W. R. Labega, Brouwer too became frustrated with the centralization of administrative power on the island of Curacao. He petitioned H. M. the Queen for a separation from Curacao with direct administration from Holland for the Windward Islands.

"Mr. Brouwer ran unsuccessfully for national office in the Legislative Council *(Staten)* in 1938 but was elected on St. Maarten as a member of the 'Court of Policy' *(Raad van Politie)*. Although he was the son of a former Governor, he was considered a radical and attracted to his camp the poorer classes of St. Maarten. His love for St. Maarten shines through all of his writings even though his ancestors came from elsewhere, and he himself was born on Saba and raised partly on St. Eustatius.

"Our admiration of 'Broechie' Brouwer does not stem from the fact that he descended from illustrious ancestors, however, or that he practiced law in the Windward Islands, or even that he published a newspaper. It is rather for his confrontation with the colonial authorities, and the harassment he suffered at their hands, which ultimately led to him being practically forced into a position to take his own life.

"*De Slag om Slag* No. 133 issued on January 22nd, 1938, had questioned the Governor-General on the fairness of the voters' lists. In No. 161 of March 12th, 1938, he announced that he would be prosecuted and surely condemned. In No. 206 of March 4th, 1939, he apologized that the paper had not appeared for the past five weeks because of his imprisonment on the island of Curacao. He went on to tell the story of: 'Our editor and the prison, in which he claimed that such a long prison term (one month) had only served to lessen his fear of imprisonment. Brouwer writes, 'Now there is not even the fear of confinement to keep us from expressing our opinions and exposing those who do wrong. ... For those who fight for fair play and justice, there is no such thing as failure and defeat. Please remember also that James Russell Lowell said, "I HONOR THE MAN WHO IS WILLING TO SINK

HALF HIS PRESENT REPUTE FOR THE FREEDOM TO THINK;

AND, HAVING THOUGHT, BE HIS CAUSE STRONG OR WEAK

WILL SINK T'OTHER HALF FOR THE FREEDOM TO SPEAK."

And this we shall continue to do.

"... Brouwer was undaunted. This was not to be the final blow, however. The electoral lists of 1937 were incomplete and were so structured as to ensure the election of the late William Rufus Plantz by the colonial establishment on Curacao, Mr. Brouwer claimed.

"The *Amigoe*, the Roman Catholic newspaper on Curacao, in no uncertain term favoured the election of Plantz over Brouwer, as the latter was looked upon as a radical. The ensuing debate over the manner in which the electoral lists had been made up raised many questions as to the validity of the candidacy of the late W. R. Plantz. At the same time it was alleged that the names of the other 'foreigners' like W. Netherwood (editor of *Bovenwindse Stemmen*) and Mr. Darrell, who had been on the island for many years, were omitted from the voters' lists. These same people had been allowed to vote and take part in the previous elections for local councilor.

"When reading *De Slag om Slag* now some fifty years later, and knowing that the colonial governors in those days had virtual dictatorial powers, one can only all the more appreciate Mr. Brouwer for his outspoken manner. On December 7th, 1939, Mr. Brouwer was found dead in his home of a bullet wound. The authorities claimed this was self-inflicted. There were others, especially among the poorer classes, who doubted it. Some felt that he had been too critical, and that he had been eliminated by the authorities.

"Prior to his death, Mr. Brouwer had been highly agitated for several weeks in connection with government plans to arrest him once again. The offense was that he had reprinted an article from a Canadian magazine which was critical of a 'friendly' head of state. Who was this 'friendly' head of state whose good name and reputation the Dutch were so concerned about? None other than Adolf Hitler of Germany. That same 'friendly' head of state invaded Holland on May 10th, 1940, and Mr. Brouwer, though too late, was vindicated.

"In some circles, Mr. Brouwer is only remembered because of his dramatic exit from the world of the living. The record of his life, however, is such that he is worthy of our highest praise and admiration. One must remember that the period in which Mr. Brouwer published his feisty newspaper was the turbulent thirties, the years prior to the Second World War. These were years in which the colonial authorities were not known for their tolerance towards opposition to their views. *De Slag om Slag* was completely opposed to the dictates handed down to the other islands by the colonial Governor-General on Curacao. Mr. Brouwer displayed exceptional courage to come out weekly in print with his views. It cannot be disputed that he gave his life for the ideas and opinions for which he fought all his life, and for this we should be grateful."

[6] Will Johnson, For The Love of St. Maarten *(New York: Carlton Press, 1987), pp. 83-86.*

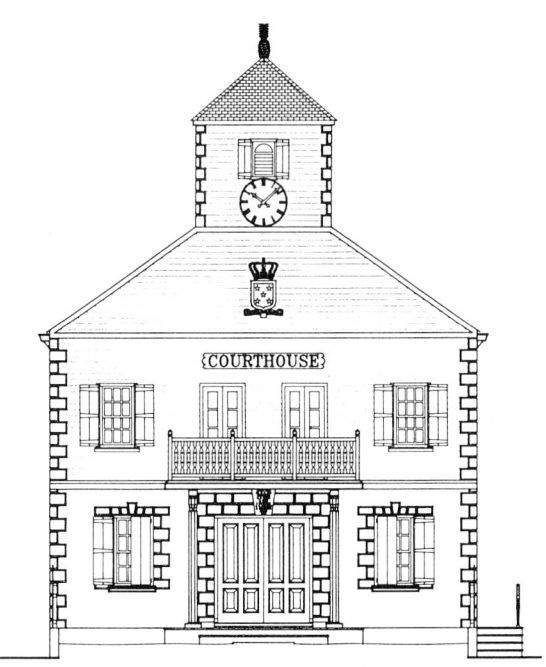

Court House where Brouwer worked. Front elvation after 1996 restoration. Source: Plan'D2.

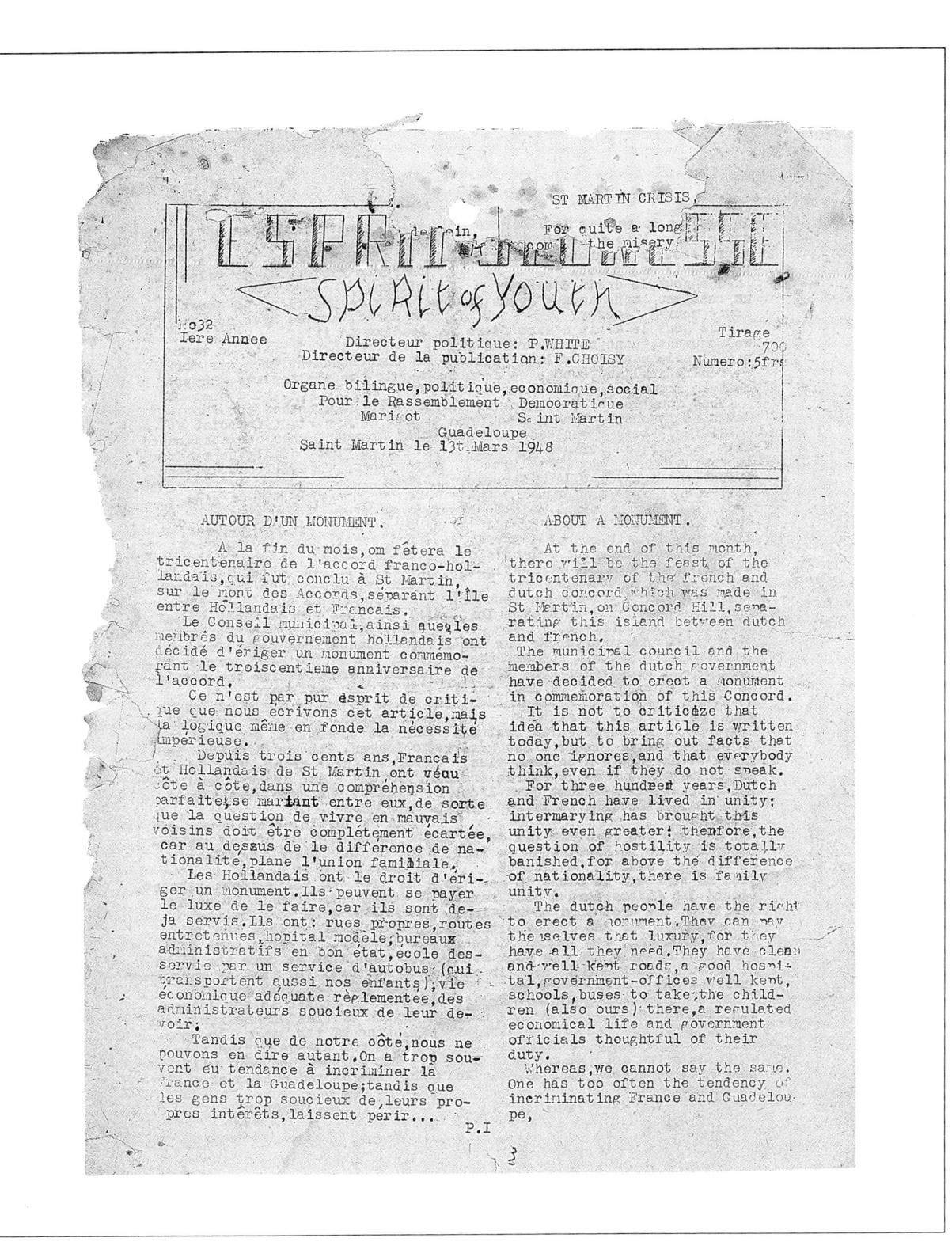

ESPRIT de la JEUNESSE
Spirit of Youth

No32
Iere Annee

Directeur politique: P.WHITE
Directeur de la publication: F.CHOISY

Tirage 700
Numero: 5frs

Organe bilingue, politique, economique, social
Pour le Rassemblement Democratique
Marigot   Saint Martin
Guadeloupe
Saint Martin le 13th Mars 1948

ST MARTIN CRISIS

For quite a long [time]... the misery...

AUTOUR D'UN MONUMENT.

A la fin du mois, on fêtera le tricentenaire de l'accord franco-hollandais, qui fut conclu à St Martin, sur le mont des Accords, séparant l'île entre Hollandais et Français.

Le Conseil municipal, ainsi que les membres du gouvernement hollandais ont décidé d'ériger un monument commémorant le troiscentième anniversaire de l'accord.

Ce n'est par pur esprit de critique que nous écrivons cet article, mais la logique même en fonde la nécessité impérieuse.

Depuis trois cents ans, Français et Hollandais de St Martin ont vécu côte à côte, dans une compréhension parfaite; se mariant entre eux, de sorte que la question de vivre en mauvais voisins doit être complètement écartée, car au dessus de la différence de nationalité, plane l'union familiale.

Les Hollandais ont le droit d'ériger un monument. Ils peuvent se payer le luxe de le faire, car ils sont déjà servis. Ils ont: rues propres, routes entretenues, hôpital modèle, bureaux administratifs en bon état, école desservie par un service d'autobus (qui transportent aussi nos enfants), vie économique adéquate règlementée, des administrateurs soucieux de leur devoir.

Tandis que de notre côté, nous ne pouvons en dire autant. On a trop souvent eu tendance à incriminer la France et la Guadeloupe; tandis que les gens trop soucieux de leurs propres intérêts, laissent périr...

P.I

ABOUT A MONUMENT.

At the end of this month, there will be the feast of the tricentenary of the french and dutch concord which was made in St Martin, on Concord Hill, separating this island between dutch and french.

The municipal council and the members of the dutch government have decided to erect a monument in commemoration of this Concord.

It is not to criticize that idea that this article is written today, but to bring out facts that no one ignores, and that everybody think, even if they do not speak.

For three hundred years, Dutch and French have lived in unity: intermarying has brought this unity even greater: thenfore, the question of hostility is totally banished, for above the difference of nationality, there is family unity.

The dutch people have the right to erect a monument. They can pay themselves that luxury, for they have all they need. They have clean and well kept roads, a good hospital, government-offices well kept, schools, buses to take the children (also ours) there, a regulated economical life and government officials thoughtful of their duty.

Whereas, we cannot say the same. One has too often the tendency of incriminating France and Guadeloupe,

Spirit of Youth, a St. Martin newspaper that appeared from 1947 to 1948.

*F*elix Choisy was a politician and patriot. He served as a first deputy mayor (1959-1977) and general councilor (1973-1979) for St. Martin (North). On June 7, 1947, Choisy founded *Esprit De La Jeunesse (Spirit of Youth)*, the "political, economic, and social" news organ of Le Rassemblement, a political party. The four-page newspaper, named by Choisy's colleague Albert Gumbs, appeared from 1947 to 1948. Paul Whit, Sr., a co-founder of Le Rassemblement, was the newspaper's political director.

Copies of the publication were found in 1993, among Whit's papers by his son Horace, himself a political activist and successful businessman. *Esprit De La Jeunesse* sustained a spirited criticism of Mayor Louis Constant Fleming's administration (1926-1949). It was thought that the publication exposed primarily the relationship of dominance between colonial France and St. Martin. Further research indicated that it was Fleming who was blamed for not defending the people of the Commune and for the lack of schools, a hospital, electricity, poor roads, and inadequate infrastructure (no wharf and harbor lights).

1915–1989

In a 1947 issue of *Esprit De La Jeunesse*, evidence of the political opposition to Fleming appeared in an editorial written by Choisy. Mayor Fleming was implicated as "One of Vichy's most desperate representatives, ... faithful to ... ideas of slavery," alleged to be aligned with ideas and practices "... of superiority of the white race," and supposedly victimized "... fishermen ... for not giving you a franc on each kilo of fish brought to market." Ironically, Fleming was instrumental in erecting the Frontier monument in 1948 to commemorate the Treaty of Concordia's tricentenary. The monument has become one of St. Martin's most visible symbols of unity. On March 13, 1948, while Choisy raised the revolutionary point that "above the difference of nationality, there is family unity" linking St. Martiners across the border, he was pointed in his criticism of the mayor: "One has too often the tendency of incriminating France and Guadeloupe, while men, only seeking their personal interest, leave the Commune run asunder, using it as a spring board to satisfy their false ambition.

"Have we the right to erect a monument, when we have no road leading to it?

"Have we the right to be proud of that monument, when our poor people are shelterless, when our sick have to go beyond that monument to be attended to?

"Have we the right to point at that monument when our abandoned children won't be able to read or understand what will be written there?" A little over two months later, for the centenary of the 1848 emancipation, the relentless *Esprit De La Jeunesse* declared: "... We must denounce those who, by economical means, are trying to enslave our brothers and destroy the fruit of the abolition of slavery.

"We must keep a keen eye upon those false philanthropists who by subtle methods try to take from us a liberty that we have acquired by so many suffrances, those who had the impudence to say under the Vichy regime ... 'I will not have to kiss the negroes' B... any more.'"

Choisy and Whit were branded communists for their political activities. They advocated the observation of Labor Day, accountable government, the liberalism of the French Revolution, and the progressive ideas and personalities of the Negritude Movement. According to Whit, with Choisy as its editor, *Esprit De*

La Jeunesse "... was a political paper because it was demanding change from the administration which was not pleasing. We protested against it. To carry through our thoughts, our aims, we needed a paper to give the people a better chance than what we had. ... I also remember later that José Lake said 'A country without an opposition is a country that is going backwards, and a country without a newspaper is like a boat without a rudder.'" *Esprit De La Jeunesse* was distributed on both sides of the island. Whit recalled with a chuckle the story of an *Esprit De La Jeunesse* distributor in French Quarter. The person was found out, after some time, to be a Fleming supporter who secretly destroyed the newspapers instead of delivering them.

Choisy was a firm believer in the traditional saying "The Gale Doesn't Stop At The Frontier." He constantly repeated or referred to this National Motto when talking about the unity of St. Martin. In a posthumous article appearing in *Newsday*, Louis Jeffry called Choisy a "prominent apostle of St. Martinism." He was a liberal champion of reason and the sound development of the "Antillean Man" or "Antillean Personality," as he referred to what was popularly known in the 1960s and 1970s as the "New Caribbean Man." Though an official in Mayor Hubert Petit's administration, Choisy was instrumental in revoking the 1960 *persona non grata* slapped on the patriot José H. Lake, Sr.. (Lake defied the ban by crossing the Frontier into the North of St. Martin to cover news and visit friends and family.)

Following his political career, Choisy became a confidant to an unprecedented number of major politicos from both parts of the nation, regardless of their political affiliation. This may be his greatest legacy and served to distinguish him as a statesman. His was an assertive and embracing, seminal St. Martin nationalism. For this he was highly respected and trusted by a wide cross-section of the community, from young progressives to old guard conservatives. Choisy was held in high esteem by members of Guadeloupe's independence movement. At the time of his death, he was a high-ranking and internationally known Free Mason. Choisy was a recipient of France's national merit award. He received the Certificate of Excellence from the St. Martin Educational and Cultural Organization in 1988.

Choisy lived and worked in Marigot. Etching: "Big Street, Marigot," by Roland Richardson.

1913-1966

𝓒arlos A. Cooks was a historian, orator, political and social organizer, Black Nationalist, and pan-Africanist. Cooks was born in the Dominican Republic of St. Martin parentage. He came "Home" to St. Martin at an early age and attended the Oranje School. As a youngster, he played with friends on the wooden "flats" which transported salt across the Great Salt Pond.

In 1929, Cooks left St. Martin for the United States of America via the Dominican Republic. When he was a youth, his father and uncle secured his initiation into the *Sacré*, the secret Haitian society that, say legend, date back to the blood-oath among Maroon warriors and Haitian revolutionaries. In New York City, he rose vigorously through the ranks of the Universal Negro Improvement Association (UNIA) during some of its most turbulent years. Cooks was knighted by a Garvey "ambassador" at age 19 and later became president of UNIA's Advance Guard Division. He was also a commissioned officer in UNIA's African Legion.

Between 1939 and the 1940 death of that twentieth century colossus Marcus Garvey, Cooks founded the *Street Speaker* magazines. As a lobbyist for Garvey in 1939, Cooks met with US senators and congressmen to support the "Bilbo Bill of Repatriation." In 1940, the St.Martiner led a nationalist delegation that met in

Washington D. C. with President Harry Truman and senators on repatriation to Africa and other liberation issues. On June 23, 1941, he founded the African Nationalist Pioneer Movement (ANPM). After Patrice Lumumba addressed the United Nations in July of 1960, the first premier of the Republic of the Congo, now Zaire, met with Cooks. Lumumba invited Cooks to the newly independent Congo to work with him. Cooks answered that his role was to organize Africans in the Caribbean and the Americas.

In 1960, the great Kwame Nkrumah also visited the USA as Ghana's first president. When he spoke in Harlem, the African nationalist father invited Cooks to share the public platform after people at the rally began chanting: "We want Carlos Cooks!" The St. Martin man brought the red, black, and green flag to the podium. His fiery oratory, characteristically "loaded with facts and energy ... stole the show." Nkrumah was very much inspired by Garvey's writings. (A photo survives with Cooks addressing the public, while seated behind him are luminaries of Black liberation, Nkrumah, Malcolm X, and Adam Clayton Powell.) Cooks, considered arrogant by some Black leaders and scholars, refused to be interviewed by the white press. He spoke Dutch, French, and Spanish and was one of Harlem's greatest "street speakers."

To writer Akua B. Weeks, "Carlos A. Cooks was a crucial link between the Black Nationalist thought of Marcus Garvey (Universal Negro Improvement Association) in the 1920s and its rebirth in the 1960s as the Black Power Movement." Cooks was known to the New York City police and kept under surveillance by the US Federal Bureau of Investigation (FBI) for his work to organize and liberate Black people. Cooks rejected the word "Negro" as "... that ominous appellation ... a term closely connected with 'nigger.'" He advocated the use of the word "Black" or "African." In Charles Parker's eulogy to the man admirers called "The Undaunted," four of Cooks's key principles were pointed out:

1 Black education to develop thoughts and ideas and actions compatible with the Black race: pride in skin color, natural hair, and race identity.

2 BUY BLACK program to create commercial awareness and activity.

3 A true concept as to what religion is and means.

4 A will to return to the glorious land from which our race was torn away—Mother Africa.

In 1935, Cooks recruited volunteers for Ethiopia in its war against Italian aggression. That same year, twenty-two-year-old Cooks took on the Italian Mafia at the Roca Bella bar, a reputed den of prostitution for white men traveling to Harlem, drug pushers, and other criminals; and supposedly protected by corrupt cops. Cooks, led a group of nationalists in a move to close the 126th Street and Lenox Avenue mafia property.

"The Nationalists planned their strategy," recorded author Robert Harris, "Cooks mounted a step ladder with all the opposition surrounding him. He began to speak on the immorality and disrespect that the Roca Bella bar was exhibiting in the community. In the words of Cooks, 'All hell broke loose when someone threw a rock. A pimp approached the ladder with his switchblade. A mounted cop on a horse drew his gun. Someone "goosed" the horse with a switchblade. The horse went up in the air; the cop fell off the horse. The Nationalists struck their blow and retreated without a scratch, or loss of a single man.' Results, one dead cop and lot of 'whipped head' caste people and the Roca Bella bar closed. Cooks was arrested and held without bail. ... The police were, however, unable to develop a case against him."

In his autobiography, Malcolm X stated that one of the reasons he attended the meetings of senior nationalists such as Cooks was to invite persons in the audience to attend the mosque where he sermonized. Malcolm, who would rise swiftly to become a "shining Prince of Black manhood," confirmed that when he arrived as an unknown Muslim minister in Harlem, the nationalists and "Buy Black!" people constituted a formidable leadership. The term "Buy Black!" referred directly to Cooks. After breaking with Elijah Muhammad, "ANPM publications ... were the dominant literature at (Malcolm X's) OAAU meetings," recalled Harris. To nationalist Elombe Brath, Malcolm "acknowledged his debt to Cooks" publically. Cooks researcher Eddie Bobo affirmed this.

In *Malcolm X: Make it Plain*, New York City police officer William DeFossett asserted that Harlem's 125th Street was the Black capital of the world. Scores of street speakers held public forum on several corners to expound the issues of the day. The only name Defossett is recorded as remembering was "a fella" at the southeast corner "by the name of Carlos Cooks" who had "some kind of African movement going on."

Carlos Cooks once wrote, "Freedom is the greatest heritage of a people and unity is its guardian."

𝒯homas E. Duruo was an orator, political and social organizer, pan-Africanist, preacher, and patriot. Duruo was a blacksmith or boiler-maker by trade. His political and social activism as a premier Garveyite or Black consciousness leader in the Dominican Republic, Aruba, and St. Martin, spanned over thirty years.

Duruo was a founding chapter member of the Universal Negro Improvement Association/African Communities' League (UNIA-ACL) in the Dominican Republic's commercial city of San Pedro de Macoris. He and other UNIA officers organized the large community of English-speaking immigrant laborers through economic, labor, political, cultural, and educational activities based on the principles of Marcus Garvey. Duruo helped to lay the foundation for the English-language school for immigrant children. He introduced a number of St. Martiners to UNIA and Garvey's teachings of economic independence, racial pride, and African or Black nationalism.

Duruo (also pronounced Derio and probably derived from Duriuex) was thought to have been among the UNIA leadership arrested in the Dominican Republic during the 1916-1924 United States' military occupation of that Caribbean country. Mercedes

1863-1949

de Coste, the Dominican-born daughter of Duruo who he called upon to speak in Spanish at UNIA parades in San Pedro de Macoris, recalled that Duruo was not arrested. "The American marine government told the Dominican government that they were plotting to overthrow the government, and they marched in—we were rehearsing for a concert—and they took us all to prison, and I spent the night there. ... My father wasn't there then ... when I told my mother to go to *(US marine official)* Colonel *(Dwight)* Huey, who I worked for ... immediately they came and they let me out, but the other people who were just as innocent as I was, they stayed there, and they had a trial but it never amounted to anything.

"It was all a make up thing to get the Dominican government against the Universal Negro Improvement Association. Some of the people were deported. ... It was a big thing, and finally it petered out because the members started falling away from it. My father moved to Aruba; his work took him there and that's where he started *(another UNIA chapter)* and had a big thing going there."

According to magazine publisher Nab Eddie Bobo, the arrest netted UNIA officers and activists. St. Martin's James Henry Cooks (father of Carlos Cooks), a UNIA leader at the time, reputedly disguised himself as a woman and boarded a US-bound ship to escape arrest and interrogation by military and police authorities in the occupied Spanish-speaking republic. Cooks, a carpenter, was responsible for constructing the UNIA building in San Pedro de Macoris on President Jiménez Street. Lorenzo Duruo confirmed that his father was not at the weekly Sunday meetings at which UNIA officers were arrested, and that Cooks did flee to the western part of the country before "escaping" to the USA. Duruo asserted that the arrest targeted primarily immigrants from the British and then Danish colonies, and he implicated a certain British official who took particular offence to UNIA activities. The British official was said then to have encouraged the "mass arrest" and subsequent deportation. The mass arrest occurred in 1923, the year of UNIA's biggest parade in the Dominican Republic.

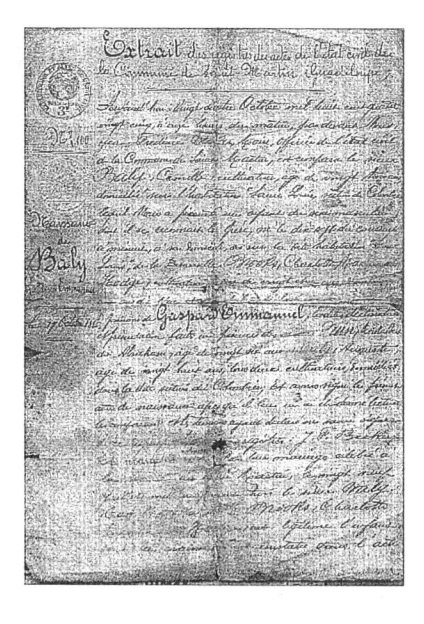

With leaders such as Victor Burnett from St. Croix in trouble and Cooks on the run, Thomas Duruo rose to the presidency of the organization. He continued the self-reliance activities, maintained the "Black Star Line building," corresponded with Garvey, and received UNIA dignitaries from abroad. US and European colonial governments and other opponents were also by 1923 reaching that "feverish pitch" which would for the next nineteen or so years contribute to the UNIA/ACL's dismantling around the world. For the rest of the twentieth century, however, the liberation ideas pioneered and galvanized by Garvey and those "race-men" or "missionaries of the race" who championed universal African redemption, grew exponentially.

During the mid-1920s, the labor situation in the Caribbean changed. The LAGO oil refinery in Aruba would make that Dutch colony the region's boom town for the next thirty-odd years. In 1927, Duruo "plunged the ocean," joining the labor-driven armada of Caribbean emigrants bound for Aruba. At the American-owned LAGO, infested with the racism of the times—(southern US white LAGO executives and managers were said to even discriminate against white St. Martiners and white Americans from northeastern states)—Duruo found employment in the maintenance department. At that time, Blacks were supposedly not employed or paid as tradesmen or department heads, especially if they had no US [...] was unofficially made a "sub-foreman" on [...]ments by a Mr. Bozard. Bozard, it is thought, [...]ean and chief of the department's work crews. [...]led "Dutch Antilles," certainly for St. Martiners [...]rtin, oral and recorded history point to Duruo [...]ury father of Black consciousness. In Aruba, [...] Burnett and others coming out of the wind- [...]ants flooding into "The Village"—then a card- [...]crate hovel in the town of San Nicolas. With [...] from non-member supporters like Diego [...]acist from either St. Vincent or Grenada, and [...]ddy" Cummings from Jamaica, Duruo headed [...]pter and the Independent Order of Ancient [...] for the remainder of the 1920s and most of

time when nothing couldn't move unless you [...]alled Lorenzo Duruo who travelled to Aruba with his father. "In Santo Domingo there was no question of French or Dutch; we were all St. Martiners and Papa believed in

---

Dear Reader,

Page 64, paragraph 2, line 13, should read:

*"... the British and **once** Danish colonies, ..."*

National Symbols of St. Martin - A Primer

HOUSE OF NEHESI PUBLISHERS
© 1996

that. When he became president in Aruba, that caused some jealousy. Some of the people from the British islands always thought that they were better educated, and when they found out Duruo was from St. Martin, they didn't like that. Some of his own St. Martin people started getting jealous of his recognition and started saying they were Dutch and he was French. ... They carried news to the Dutch police and detectives. When Elias Richardson came to work with the police, they said he was one of them (*St. Martiners with Dutch nationality*), so they carried news to him." Richardson met Duruo and eventually became a UNIA stockholder.

Duruo was able to keep the people from the different islands together because "he believed the Black Star Line was for everybody, all Black people. The Dutch couldn't get him to sell out ... and after the Dutch police captain got to know who Duruo was, he would come around ... to talk; and Papa would find out the names of some of the people who were carrying news. But whenever people came from abroad or they needed a recommendation, they came to Duruo." He continued to look for jobs at LAGO and attend other concerns for St. Martiners and other Caribbean peoples, whether their colonial "nationality" was Dutch, French, Danish, or British. Apparently, much of the news-carrying and snitching had more to do with smuggling of goods and other illegalities in The Village than with UNIA political and social organizing.

When he retired in his native St. Martin, Duruo continued to advocate racial pride and self-reliance. Cole Bay grocer and Duruo admirer, Xaviar van Buren James, recalled that "Duruo got in the ropes with the French authorities" for his activities. The late "Sage of Marigot Hill," Theopilus Priest, said in 1987, that Duruo, his Garveyite teacher, was "a brave, intelligent man."

Generally well-respected at "Home," Duruo held regular "church meetings" under an ancient tamarind tree in the yard of his Rambaud home. A devoted Catholic, tolerant of all peoples, and well-read in world history and current affairs, Duruo sermonized on the relationship between religion, history, politics, economics, race, and the "upliftment" of St. Martiners and Black people everywhere. Assisted by his granddaughter Thomassillienne Arnell, he also taught children and adults to read and write during the early 1940s. His late daughter Julie Arnell exclaimed in a 1982 interview how "... Papa love he Black people!"

The IOAC probably influenced Duruo's religious thought as much as the *World Almanac* and UNIA's *Negro World* informed him on world affairs. Visiting IOAC officers introduced to Duruo in Aruba by Williamson were impressed by his leadership, intellectual, and oratory qualities. They asked him to open a lodge chapter, made him an honorary member, and presented him with, among other books, *The Lost Books of the Bible*. The new knowledge and information must have fired the already focused intellect regarding the key role of Blacks and Africa in biblical and world history. Lorenzo Duruo felt that this was "the big thing" his father preached during his latter years in Aruba from the second floor of the "Black Star Line building." This information must have been central to the freedom fighter's "church meetings" in Rambaud. Sometimes St. Martiners from the South leaving a Duruo meeting were "escorted" to the border by French authorities. Garveyite L. B. Scott was one well-known St. Martiner who it is said had such an experience. Felix Choisy considered Duruo to be one of the three great orators of twentieth century St. Martin.

In 1987, the Marcus Garvey Centennial Award was bestowed on Thomas Emmanuel Duruo posthumously.

*1*8₉₈–*1*9₈₈

*M*elford A. Hazel was a farmer, trader, pioneer hotelier, taxi driver, and Island Council member. Influenced by the economic principles of Marcus Garvey, Hazel, up to the time of his death, was a role model for many St. Martiners aspiring to own a successful business. The flagship of Hazel's enterprise, the Seaview Beach Hotel, was opened with two floors and eleven rooms as the island's first modern hotel in 1948. (Passangrahan opened as an inn in 1902.) In 1996, the three-story, fifty-room Seaview Beach Hotel building is still located on Frontstreet and owned by the Hazel family. Further testimony to Hazel's industry is the significant number of his descendants who own and operate successful businesses.

Hazel was one of the first Black St. Martiners to own property in Great Bay, the traditional name for Philipsburg. Among Hazel's holdings in over fifty years of business included a grocery shop (which provided home deliveries), a bakery, and an ice and lemonade factory. He loaned money to help men and women open small shops in Dutch Quarter, Cole Bay, and elsewhere when the bank, and before that, wealthier families, would not.

A little known fact about Hazel is that he was a sea-going trader or smuggler who captained his own boat. According to reporter Lloyd Richardson, "Due to the times (World War II) and the intentions for the smuggled goods, the dangerous profession was considered an honorable one and earned him the recognition as a hero-of-sorts by many St. Maarteners who coveted the cargo of provisions and commodities that were then 'like gold' on the island." Most of the precious cargo was bought on the high seas from Hazel's "friend" who sailed out of St. Thomas. Both men risked encounters with German submarines patrolling the ocean bottom to, among other reasons, disrupt Allied fuel supply.

In 1951, as leader of Southern St. Martin's Democratic Party, Hazel was elected to the first modern Island Council's single opposition seat. When he led St. Martin's Nationale Volkspartij (NVP) "chapter" in 1955, Hazel was not re-elected to the Island Council. One year earlier, "Curaçao and its dependencies" obtained the autonomy *Statuut* within the colonial Dutch Kingdom, as "The Netherlands Antilles."

Hazel's retreat from active politics did not stop his social involvement, however. He was a founding member of the Oranje Benevolent Improvement Association, an off-shoot of the Philipsburg Mutual Improvement Association. PMIA and OBIA were influenced by the Universal Negro Improvement Association. Daughter Eulalie Meyers has added to the pioneer's social achievements through her leadership in church and community organizations. Son Sam Hazel and grandsons Charles and Frankie Meyers would follow the old man's footsteps into politics.

In 1987, Hazel was a recipient of the Marcus Garvey Centennial Award. Before his death in 1988, the Hazel patriarch was inducted into the Dutch royal house for his outstanding service to St. Martin in particular and the Antillean community in general.

The Melford A. Hazel Road can be found at the Ebenezer Estate Housing Development.

Joseph H. Lake, Sr., was a pioneer journalist, politician, publisher, labor organizer, orator, and patriot. On Emancipation Day, July 1, 1959, José Lake, as he was widely known, founded the *Windward Islands Opinion* newspaper "... as a means of helping to improve the social, economic, educational, and political conditions of the Windward Islands by advocating against the causes of Injustice and Oppression."

Lake's writings exposed government neglect and corruption, criticized what he called "slave wages" in the public and private sector, and advanced progressive ideas about self-pride and democracy. To writer Camille Baly, Lake must be counted among St. Martin's early trade union advocates and activists. He was the first to publically advocate for better wages and facilities for the pier and Landsradio workers during the early 1960s. Attorney Roland Duncan asserted that during election campaigns, candidate Lake's approach was the most modern and independent the island had seen up to the early 1970s. His emphasis was on organization and issues, regardless of his political party affiliation or alliance. The journalistic and political work of José Lake placed him in immediate conflict with the establishment on both sides of the island. His consistently toughest bouts were, however, with the political and economic bosses in the South. For much of the 1960s and early 1970s, he was the leading, and at times the only, vocal and visible opposition to the absolute rule of Claude Wathey and his Democratic Party (DP) machine. This earned Lake the name "Dean of the Political Opposition."

A firm believer in the historical unity of St. Martin and the socio-cultural oneness of her people, Lake wrote and fought against exploitation and discrimination in the North and South of his "Sweet St. Martin Land." In 1960, Lake was declared *persona non grata* by French law, banning him from traveling to the North because he had written articles condemning the French colonial education system for keeping St. Martin's children backward. He took photographs of deplorable class-room conditions and called on Mayor Hubert Petit to correct them. That same year, in a dispatch to St. Croix's WIVI radio, the intrepid journalist accused Mayor Hubert Petit of attempting to "... suppress freedom of press by intimidating Editor *(of the) Windward Islands' Opinion*," and holding "... a mass meeting on Sunday, October ninth, to incite people to violence against Editor." One political leader told the crowd that anyone who saw Lake on the "Frenchside" could shoot him.

1925 — 1976

Lake refused to be intimidated, defied the ban, and declared that as a St. Martiner he was free to go anywhere on his island.

On October 9, 1960, Lake received a letter from Lt. Governor Jan Jacob Beaujon (1959-1968), warning that the mayor could not guarantee Lake's life "on the Frenchside." Mayor Petit further accused Lake of indulging in "subversive" activities. Incidentally, Lake and Beaujon clashed in a 1968 Island Council meeting over Beaujon's alleged racist remarks or proposal to breed Japanese men with St. Martin's Black women to create the "Jaego" or "Jaegro" race ("Jaegro" from the words "Japanese" and "negro").

In the 1963 Island Council election, Lake was a candidate of the Nationale Volkspartij (NVP-St. Martin). The NVP list was headed by L. B. Scott, but Lake received the party's highest number of votes. (It is rare in St. Martin's politics for a party leader to receive fewer votes in an election than other candidates on the party's list.) According to political scientist Joseph H. Lake, Jr., in his notes from a 1974 interview, José Lake said that the party's leadership reneged on a gentleman's agreement to send its candidate with the most votes to the Island Council. Scott was seated as the opposition's sole Island Council member.

Throughout the early 1960s, Lake was mocked and spat upon by the ruling DP supporters when he gave election campaign speeches to his supporters in Great Bay (Philipsburg). Businessman Leo Friday committed to memory a confrontation between Lake and Wathey following a disruption at one of Lake's political rallies. Wathey was brought into the meeting in dramatic fashion. Many of the people seated in the Oranje School meeting area that night scampered away at the entrance of the political boss, braced on the shoulders of two male DP "die-hards." The sight of adults running away like frightened children at the entry of one man propped on two shoulders like a slave master of yore must have pierced Lake's heart and mind like a poisonous arrow. Lake, said Friday, pointed to Wathey and stoutly declared: "Claude Wathey, why are you doing this? One day these people are going to be called upon to become independent. Why are you doing this to my people? Don't ride my people!"

It was no easier for Lake to sell his newspaper. According to Felix Choisy, St. Martiners hid in the alleys or *steegjes* of Great Bay to buy the *Opinion*. Some hid it in a brown paper bag, in their shirt or blouse, and hurried away. It was an unwritten political offense to be caught reading what was then the island's only newspaper. Lake was regularly taunted by opponents when he drove through Great Bay with shouts of "Outta Town, José Lake, outta Town!" He was forced to arm himself after having been threatened numerous times for his reporting and political activism. The hostile atmosphere peaked with the burning of the *Opinion's* and People's Printery office on the night of August 25, 1966. The fire is still thought to have been politically motivated. It remains questionable, however, whether it was the opposition or establishment forces that instigated the fire. Indeed, by 1965, noted Saba's Senator Will Johnson, the opposition had also betrayed Lake. During the 1960s, José Lake popularized the phrases which were revived during the heightened political awareness and street demonstrations of the late 1980s and early 1990s: "Long Live The People. The People United Will Never Be Defeated," and "Only The People Can Save The People." He would raise his fist above his head and punctuate his speeches with these phrases.

José Lake tirelessly encouraged the people of St. Martin, especially young people, to pursue the highest possible education and to take great pride in being St. Martiners and in being Black men and women. In the 1960s, along with the then young school teacher Camille Baly, Lake led the charge against the practice of Zwarte Piet terrorizing school children during the Christmas season. According to Baly, Lake called the practice racist and psychologically damaging to the self-esteem of St. Martin's children. Lake wrote strongly against the racist symbol of Zwarte Piet in the *Opinion* until outrage was heard from the very pulpit. The activity was consequently banned from the schools. The crusading newsman was also influential in stopping the practice of tourists throwing coins off the small pier in Great Bay for children to dive into the sea and retrieve the coins. He said it was training St. Martin's children to be beggars.

During Lake's early days of political activism, there were people who verbally abused him or tore his always impeccably pressed shirt at political campaign rallies. According to Friday, Lake's answer to those who asked why he accepted such treatment was simply, "They're my people; they don't understand yet that I am fighting for them."

In 1966, to the great consternation and disappointment of opposition forces, Lake took part in the central government election as a Democratic Party candidate. In a 1974 *Shaka* interview, Lake stated that Aruban politico and friend, Ernesto O. Petronia,

```
Vol. 1                                    Editor: J. H. Lake
No. 5                                             Middle Region.
Published every
Wednesday                                         Wednesday
Printers: The People's Printery                   July 29, 1959.
Price per copy in the W.I. Fls. 0.15
Elsewhere Fls. 0.25      LABOUR CONQUERS ALL THINGS.
```

TWENTY-FIVE YEARS IN THE SERVICES OF GOD.   MISS MARGORIE RICHARDSON BACK HOME.

of Partido Patriotico Arubano (PPA) asked him "... to join with Claude Wathey and give him a helping hand. Thinking that Claude meant well, I joined him with the expectation that I would have been able to get something tangible done in the social and cultural field." Consolidating DP and opposition forces on St. Martin appeared to have been more in the interest of guaranteeing a parliamentary or Staten election victory.

Lake and Petronia thought such a victory would effect greater Antillean-wide democratic change. Lake was convinced that he had taken up the challenge because "Most of the material things for which I had been fighting were realized." Now he had a better chance of proposing or helping to develop social, economic, and educational policies and structures to involve St. Martin's people in the island's advancement. He also took part in the 1969 parliamentary election as a DP candidate.

Following the labor-led uprising of May 30, 1969, which destroyed Willemstad in a riotous blaze, and the ensuing election, Lake's ally, Petronia, emerged as prime minister of The Netherlands Antilles. Petronia was the first Black man to become prime minister of the then six-island "constellation." Universal suffrage was instituted in 1948. Until that time, the only Black man to lead the six "island territories" in their over three hundred years as a Dutch colonial unit with a Black majority population, was Dr. M. F. da Costa Gomez (May 1949-July 1949) as president of the General Governing Council. According to Lake, Wathey was instrumental in pressuring politicians in Willemstad during the 1969 central government formation to select Petronia as prime minister.

In 1967, extending the reason for running with DP in the Staten election, Lake remained with the party of his old rival for the Island Council election. The "Bold and Brave" warrior's absence from the opposition ranks had apparently so depleted the anti-government leadership that the election was uncontested. The DP went into office unchallenged. In 1971, he again ran for the Island Council. Internal DP conflict about his position as the number two candidate on the electoral list caused Lake to place himself at the bottom of the list—to seek election by preferential votes. He received the DP's second highest amount of votes but fell a few votes short of electing himself. He was subsequently appointed Public Relations Officer for the Island Government.

Whether seated in the Island Council or through the pages of the *Opinion*, Lake continued to champion what he called "The Cause That Be." The people's politician eventually found it impossible to effect progressive change through the Wathey-dominated DP: "I became convinced that Claude Wathey was not interested in defending the rights of the working man, but only of a small group of businessmen." The "small group of businessmen" refused to advertise in Lake's newspaper, often on the advice of leading politicians and because of the *Opinion's* defense of workers against exploitation. The business boycott of the *Opinion* (which extended to its successor *Newsday*) was instrumental in keeping Lake economically weak.

Lake and Wathey, as "popular" politicians, constituted the duality of St. Martin's post-1963 political culture. Both sons-of-the-soil generated a dialectic dominance in shaping the foundation of modern politics in St. Martin (North and South) which remained influential at the time of this writing. Wathey's political strength, effected significantly by his family's wealth, was consolidated through the Democratic Party "machine." Lake remained economically disadvantaged but motivated by principles. He never stopped appealing to his people with progressive ideals to develop their pride, education, and self-reliance. Both politicians, in their "eternal" conflict, were typically non-conservative and non-elitist. What Lake cited as Wathey's retarding paternalism, however, stood in stark contrast to the "people's liberation" philosophy the independent "newspaper man" expounded from the pages of the *Opinion* and the political platform.

In October 1972, Lake founded the Christian Democratic Party (CDP), which changed its name in 1974, to the United

People's Liberation Front. In the 1973 Staten election, CDP ran a combined list with Windward Islands People's Movement (WIPM), headed by Jocelyn A. Arndell. After 1973, Lake and his followers were called "The Bold and The Brave."

In 1974, Lake stated that he was "fully in favor of an independent Netherlands Antilles," with increased autonomy for each island "to handle its own internal affairs." He was "ashamed" that "most of our politicians are afraid of Independence." Between 1959 and 1974, pointed out Johnson, "... Mr. Joseph H. Lake ... in his *Windward Islands Opinion* and in his political career repeatedly called on the authorities at Curacao to loosen their reigns on the Windward Islands."

José Lake's political and journalistic experience was not limited to St. Martin or the Windward Islands. In 1955, he was elected to Aruba's Island Council on the PPA slate. A founding member of the NWIWA ("St. Maarten Club") in 1944, and later of PPA's "autonomous" Windward Islands section, politician Leo Chance said that Lake, his political mentor, was a primary social and political mover in Aruba's Windward Islands community during PPA's heyday. The Windward Islanders were rallied by their community leaders into a bloc vote which was key in clinching PPA's first election victory in the 1950s. Lake, D. Mathew, and others lobbied for their home islands through PPA's man in the central government, Juancho E. Yrausquin. As Minister of Finance (1958-1962), Yrausquin was instrumental in delivering a number of long-awaited development projects requested by the Windward Islands. Chance, Mathew, Carl Anslijn, and Hugh Lopes were among the principal political figures in Aruba's Windward Islands community (Lake, Chance, and Mathew were called "The three musketeers").

At the American-owned LAGO oil refinery in Aruba, Lake worked as a poster in the Storehouse Department. He was a key member of LAGO Employee Council (LEC) and an assistant editor of *LAGO Employee Council News* (an English/Papiamentu newspaper). In 1957, Island Councilman Lake was accepted to Cornell University's School of Industrial and Labor Relations on a Teagle Foundation Scholarship. He was denied a United States of America visa because of a previous court fine of fifty guilders for writing an article in *LEC News* defending a LAGO worker. The employee was suspended by an American "administrator." In the article, the "administrator" was referred to as "The Big Chief with the intelligence of a 12-year-old boy scout." Lake's contemporaries believed there was a conspiracy to prevent the 32-year-old St. Martiner from studying labor relations, particularly after his run-in with "Big Chief." Neither did he hide his intentions to "go to America to study labor relations and come back to organize the LAGO workers."

Closer to "Home," Lake was instrumental in bringing Anguilla's decisive struggle to secede from the St. Kitts-Nevis-Anguilla associated state to the international media. Between 1967 and 1969, Lake filed reports for Reuters on the rebellion within the three-island British colony. The Anguillan secessionists were fed up with the historical "domination" and neglect from a centralized colonial administration in Basseterre, St. Kitts. Anguillans demanded "local" self-administration. A senior British civil servant was dispatched from London and installed in The Valley as a temporary administrator. (Between 1979 and 1980, Anguilla was officially separated from the colonial polity of St. Kitts-Nevis-Anguilla. In 1983, St. Kitts & Nevis became an independent country.) Photographer Wilfred Roumou recalled that he and Lake were detained briefly at gun point in Anguilla by British troops. Lake, Jr., added in a 1993 "Antillean Press Day" statement, that the senior Lake was physically pushed around by British soldiers while he was covering the height of the crisis in 1969. The colonial soldiers were deployed by Britain in 1969, after the British administrator was routed by the Anguillans that same year.

The famed Kittitian political patriarch Robert L. Bradshaw was vilified by the Anguillan population during the crisis, and he was said to be at odds with Lake's reporting. However, both men would in 1970 become steadfast friends during Lake's coverage of the Christina ferryboat disaster in which many people drowned in the turbulent waters of the St. Kitts/Nevis channel. Premier Bradshaw delivered a moving address at Lake's funeral.

José Lake, like many St. Martiners of his generation, was born in the Dominican Republic. At the age of five, he was brought "Home" to his mother's native village of Middle Region. Lake attended St. Joseph School (in 1988, one of his daughters, Carmen Bowers-Lake, would become the first St. Martin principal of the primay school in some one hundred years). In his late teens, already a member of the Universal Negro Improvement Association and Philipsburg Mutual Improvement Association, Lake sailed to Aruba to further his education and to find work.

By the time Lake died in 1976, he had emerged as a most beloved son-of-the-soil, a patriot, and freedom-fighter who selflessly championed the cause of St. Martin's people. He had a personable disposition which made him approachable to many, endeared him passionately to those who knew him well, and enabled him to remain on good speaking terms with his most ardent political opponents. Lake was a Rotarian and a "worshipful grand master" with the Adrien C. Richardson masonic lodge (Prince Hall affiliation). In addition to English, he wrote and spoke fluent Dutch, French, Papiamentu, and Spanish. José H. Lake, Sr.'s funeral was the largest the island had recorded at that time and the first, and only to date, to receive a full-length island-wide radio broadcast. One regional magazine likened it to a state funeral and called it unusual for a Caribbean journalist. Two Master's theses are dedicated to his memory. A 1993 University of Florida graduate thesis by Christopher Blaise Harig, purported that the founding of Lake's *Opinion* and PJD-2 radio in 1959 were central to introducing an era of great change for St. Martin. In the 1996 Carnival Calypso Competition, Lake was cited as a St. Martin hero in the song of master kaisonian "Mighty Brat." Calypso Barbara sang to his honor in an earlier Carnival tune. Poems have also been dedicated to him. The John Cooper/José Lake, Sr., Ball Park in Cul-de-Sac, and the José H. Lake, Sr. Road at Ebenezer Estate Housing Development bear the patriot's name.

In the 1987 book, *For the Love of St. Maarten*, Johnson wrote about his old friend and mentor: "Lake's contributions to St. Maarten were many. ... His political career did not achieve for him a position where he could help his people. But he did inspire me and others to write and fight. ... He established a lively free press in the Windward Islands. He made the younger generation aware of the role played by Black people in the history of the world. He also pinpointed many of the ills in the St. Maarten society which were not attended to and which have taken on epidemic proportions in recent years."

In 1994, thirty-five years after the founding of the *Opinion*, a commemorative stamp bearing the image of Joseph Husurell Lake, Sr., was issued by The Netherlands Antilles Postal Service for his meritorious work to the St. Martin and Antillean communities. The stamp sold out in record time.

Nina

Nina Larmonie-Duverly was a school principal in Guadeloupe before retiring in St. Martin. She then opened a trade school. Larmonie-Duverly devoted herself to the drop-outs and young people who could not afford to leave St. Martin to further their education. For a few years she operated a pre-school center. Later, this committed and far-sighted educationist donated her school building to the boyscouts.

After her death in 1982, a primary school in Marigot was named in Nina Larmonie-Duverly's honor.

1916-1982

1812

Francois A. Perrinon was a soldier, abolitionist, labor reformer, and businessman. He was born in Saint Pierre, Martinique. His great-grandmother, a native of the Guinea area in West Africa, was kidnapped, shipped to the Caribbean in chains, and sold as a slave.

Perrinon, whose father was a Frenchman, rose through the military ranks to become a commander in the French navy. In May 1845, his writings were published in the French Naval Annals under the heading "Results and Experiences in Slave Labor." His ideas about wage labor versus slavery appear to have been developed primarily in St. Martin. He set up the Saltponds Company of St. Martin in the South and a like venture in the North to exploit the salt-pans between 1844 and 1861. He owned salt-pans in Grand Case before 1848.

According to historian Daniella Jeffry, Perrinon was a member of the Paris-based Society for the Abolition of Slavery. Founded in 1843, to replace *Amis des Noirs*, the Society was chaired by the famed Victor Schoelcher. Perrinon fought to institute wage labor in St. Martin and put an end to the inhuman system of slavery. He refused to own slaves and paid the Black men and women who worked in his salt-pans. This was a revolutionary and practically seditious act in his time. Schoelcher supposedly used Perrinon's ideas about the benefits of wage labor over slavery as some of the stronger arguments for the abolition of the unholy institution. As undersecretary in France's temporary government following the February Revolution of 1848, Schoelcher was instrumental in passing the law to abolish slavery in France's Caribbean colonies.

1861

There is an unsubstantiated tale that goes like this: When slavery was abolished in the French colonies on May 27, 1848, the plantation owners and overseers in St. Martin kept the news from the enslaved people. It was Perrinon, some say, returning probably from Guadeloupe or Martinique in July, who wholly confirmed what the enslaved population was hearing piecemeal, that "massa day" was done. Perrinon is not mentioned in the Emancipation song. That historic song does record that slave masters, overseers, government, and church officials in St. Martin tried to hide the emancipation news from our enslaved ancestors, and that the people were aware of this deception.

Ten years after emancipation, Perrinon had not abandoned St. Martin and her people in freedom as did many planters and salt-pan owners who had abused her humanity during slavery. On August 20, 1859, Perrinon wrote to Dutch Minister of Interior Affairs, Baron J. van Cets van Guadriaan. He sought support for "the cession of the Philipsburg saltpond." Perrinon was "persuaded," though within the context of colonialism, that St. Martin, then "the poorest of all the Dutch colonies," could be rescued from "this abandonment ... by trade and navigation" and turned into "a very important island in the archipelago of the Caribbean."

It is suspected that Perrinon died by poisoning, by conspiring remnants of planters and salt-pan owners. After 1848, the colonial rulers of St. Martin continued to oppose his ideas, plans, and efforts to pay the Black people better wages for their labor and thereby raise the living standards. Perrinon made St. Martin his home and engaged principles and practices of business that advanced the dignity and well-being of her people. He is buried in the Marigot Cemetery.

*A*lrett B. Peters is the father of modern St. Martin's trade unionism. In the late 1960s, Peters organized the St. Martin Taxi Drivers Association. Later, he extended his union activities into other sectors and formed the General Workers Union. He served as the first president of both unions. This indomitable trade unionist traveled throughout the Caribbean and the United States of America to study trade unionism and meet with labor leaders.

1924—   In the early 1970s, Peters was a founder of the *Labor Spokesman* which advocated trade unionism. The short-lived newspaper joined the *Windward Islands Opinion* in calling for greater autonomy for St. Martin (South), Saba, and St. Eustatius from the central government in Willemstad.

1985

Peters led the first successful stevedore strike in St. Martin. In 1971, the labor leader led taxi drivers on a strike that practically blockaded the island's Southern capital of Great Bay. The threat of a general strike in support of the taxis was hovering over the polity after it appeared that the island government was still about to go ahead and impose a license plate fee for taxis. Not only was a cruiseliner visiting at the time but the very tourism industry was just getting off the ground. Attorney Roland Duncan, then transportation secretary for the government, remembered that the tax was not imposed because of the protest. Peters, a Cole Bay native was at one time a member of the government's Advisory Council on Economic and Social Affairs. The union leader spoke fluent Papiamentu, English, Dutch, and Spanish.

Peters began his taxi-driving career in Aruba, after he was "forced out" of LAGO for being among those organizing workers when LAGO began automating. He was, before returning "Home" between 1963 and 1964, a key voice among Aruba's taxi drivers.

The trade unionist advocated more economic self-reliance and union investments in tour operations to benefit the private transportation workers of St. Martin's tourism industry. In his view, tourism was going to succeed in a big way, and he wanted his colleagues to get in on the ground floor as a group. A group would have greater economic resources. When he was unable to get enough fellow taxi drivers to invest in a jointly-owned tour company, he established his own, the St. Maarten Taxi Drivers Enterprise.

The successes of a young labor leader, Rene Richardson and a fledgling Windward Islands Federation of Labor (WIFOL) during the first half of the 1970s, were facilitated by the pioneering work of Alrett B. Peters.

*19*12
*19*81

*W*allace B. Peterson was eulogized at his funeral as a *"raconteur par excellence"* by Richard Gibson, a leading St. Martin attorney. Twelve years later, another lawyer, Roland Duncan, recalled how Peterson confounded visiting Dutch judges and lawyers in the courtroom with his knowledge of the law, though he had no formal training or degrees in jurisprudence.

Peterson returned to St. Martin around 1956, a retired sub-inspector from the Antillean Police Force (KPNA) in Curacao.

In St. Martin, he became an executive assistant to the lieutenant governor's office during the term of Johannes Christiaan Paap. Court records show that Peterson represented his first client in 1965. That year, he defended sixteen cases. Word of his appearances in court did not take long to spread on an island with a population of no more than ten thousand people. Peterson became widely known as "The Bush Lawyer," a moniker he earned for representing mostly poor people in court, and perhaps because he had no law school training. While the nickname "The Bush Lawyer" may evoke the image or mystique of a rugged, pioneer character, Peterson's knowledge of the law was based on his years of experience as a police officer, detective, and lieutenant governor's assistant.

Before venturing to "practice law," Peterson headed the

two-member list of a short-lived political party that contested the 1963 Island Council election. In the central government election of 1966, "The Bush Lawyer" ran as a Nationale Volkspartij (St. Martin) candidate. In the 1979 Island Council election, he was a Democratic Party candidate. In the early 1960s, pointed out poet/writer Charles Borromeo Hodge, Peterson was "for years a sworn disciple of José Lake." His political activities during the mid to late 1960s were not without controversy. However, the lawman would not be remembered much for political activism.

Peterson's critical role in securing legal representation for the poor may be inferred from the following memorial address by colleague and friend Gibson: "'Pete', as his friends called him, has cause to look back on a colorful and adventurous life. Many an anecdote was told and retold by him of his many years in the police corps, especially the years he had served as a detective, during which he gained the respect and admiration of all his colleagues. Detective work, even after he left the corps, was very dear to Pete. His advice and help were regularly sought. Pete was a *raconteur par excellence*, and his humor and wit made friends seek his company and kept foes at abeyance.

"Pete's linguistic ability was put to excellent use during the past 20 years in exercising his profession as a 'legal practitioner.' His 20 years in exercising his services were virtually rendered *Pro Deo* for humanitarian reasons. The unfortunate could always count on Pete to champion its cause. Pete was known by his colleagues as the 'walking encyclopedia.' Call a name of a person on St. Maarten, and Pete would be able to recite that person's whole family tree. Ask Pete about a piece of land, and Pete could give you, *stante pede*, a complete history of that land, going back to its original owner. Indeed, he was a Census Office and a Cadastre Office all in one.

"On Friday, March 20th—the day Pete passed away—the Court, under case Nr. 5, had scheduled Marianna Peterson, represented by WALLACE BRADFORD PETERSON, against the RENT COMMISSION. Pete appeared and pleaded his case as he had done so often in the past. In the evening, at home with his wife and family, Pete rehearsed, as he so loved to do, the fine points of that case against the Rent Commission. Immediately hereafter, Pete was no more. He had pleaded and rehearsed his last earthly case.

"Pete's case has been put to rest. His memory, however,

shall live on in and out of the courts of Sint Maarten."

At the time of his death, Peterson was a practicing *zaakwaarnemer* or solicitor with the Gibson and Duncan law firm for over one decade. Before joining what would become the nation's most prestigious law firm, "The Bush Lawyer" had his own practice throughout the 1960s. During his years of appearing before the court, Peterson was the *zaakwaarnemer* for four hundred and fifty-nine cases. His first and last court appearances involved rent issues.

The W. B. Peterson Road is located in the Ebenezer Estate Housing Development.

Simpson Bay (ca anno 1920)

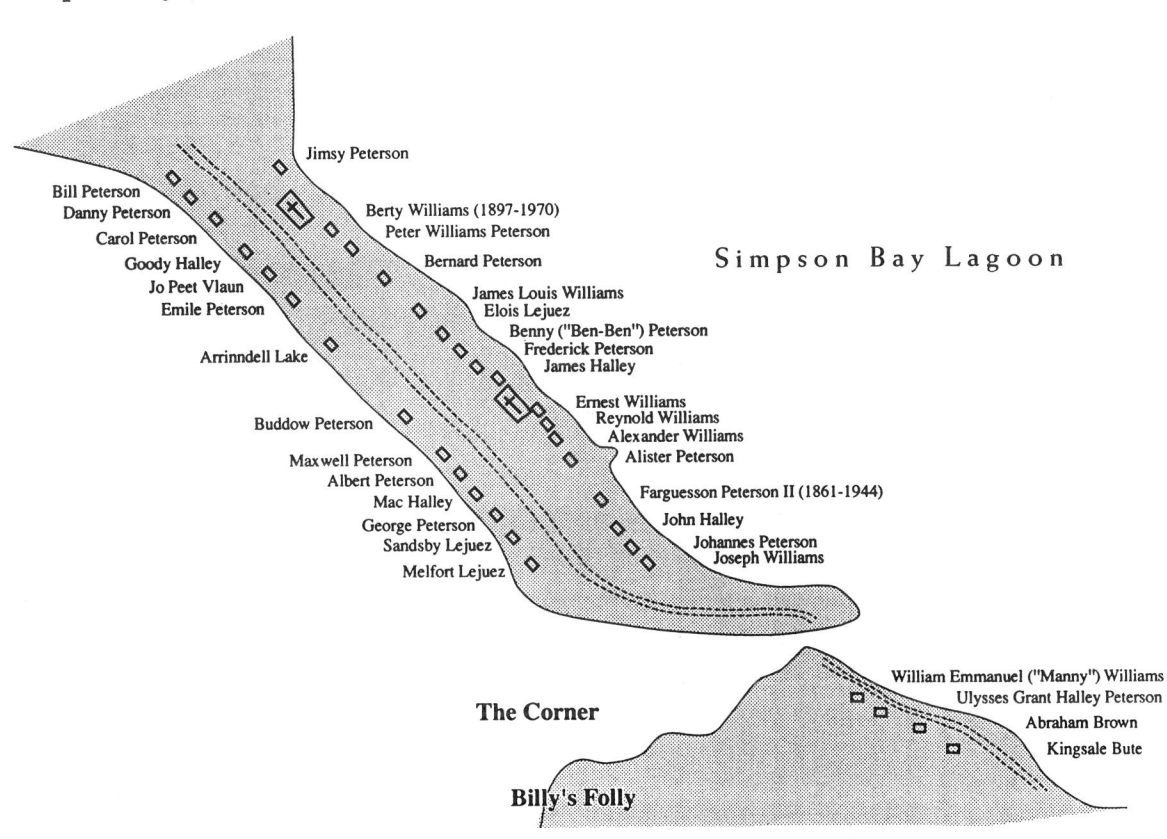

Simpson Bay families around 1920. Simpson Bay and Grand Case are St. Martin's traditional fishing villages. Source: St. Maarten Since Columbus: The First Centuries.

1926-1981

Alberic Aurelien Richards, born on April 26, 1926, in Cripple Gate, St. Martin, was a sportsman, civil servant, and politician.

"Bric," as Richards was called by many of his friends and political supporters, began his public career at the *Etat Civil* in the Mairie (government administration building) in Marigot. At this government department where births, deaths, marriages, and census data are registered, Richards started helping people to understand the French political system. He was one of the few public servants trusted by the historically English-speaking St. Martiners to write confidential letters in French to government authorities and to translate official French language documents. As an ardent football player and sports organizer from an early age, Richards spent much time on the football field teaching players to read. He eventually opened a bookshop.

According to Alex Richards, director of the Municipal Library in Marigot, his father was very much influenced by U.S. Civil Rights leader, Dr. Martin Luther King, Jr., and entered active politics in the late 1960s to further help his people. At that time, it was still financially difficult for any significant number of Black St. Martiners to run for political office, and consequently near impossible to be elected as mayor, general councilor, or to any other position of political leadership.

After campaigning unsuccessfully against Mayor Hubert Petit and Felix Choisy for the General Council seat in the late 1960s and early 1970s, Bric entered into a political alliance with former mayor Elie Fleming. The wealthy Fleming, descendant of an old political family, had been trying for years to unseat the Petit administration. The Fleming/Richards alliance, compounded by Bric's hard-nosed political approach and an endearing appeal, secured a 1979 General Council election victory. Alberic Richards was seated in the General Council, located in Basseterre, Guadeloupe. In the 1977 mayoral election, the Fleming/Richards alliance defeated the once extremely popular incumbent mayor, Hubert Petit. General Councilor Richards was appointed first deputy mayor in Mayor Elie Fleming's administration.

Bric was a very bold and confident politician who incessantly challenged his opposition. Campaign assistants recalled that he would tell his opponents, "I'm going to beat you on Sunday!" (French elections are held on Sundays.) He never believed he could lose an election, and when he did lose at the ballot box, Bric started campaigning the following day for the next election. Despite long hours away from his family, Bric is remembered by his children as "a real family man." He was loved by his people, and he loved his people and island. A staunch believer in honor, Richards attempted to set an example of how the political apparatus could be used to create a better St. Martin for all St. Martiners.

On August 28, 1981, Alberic Áurelien Richards passed away in a Guadeloupe hospital—ten days after celebrating his twenty-fifth wedding anniversary. It is often the case with great men and women who become an enigma or threat to the status quo because of their popularity, principles, and commanding presence to engender popular or "radical" change, that their death is hard to accept by the people who, through their heroes' grand vision, glimpse a brighter future. So, as with Francois Perrinon, "Broechie" Brouwer, and Bric's close friend José Lake, Sr., Richards's death is still looked upon by some supporters and family members as an unsolved mystery. The "dirty hands" are said to belong to "the powers that be"—because of Bric's supposed aspiration to run for the post of mayor. "I surely believe he has left this earth with a few untold stories," said Alex Richards in a 1993 interview with "Conscious Lyrics" radio program host Alex Reiph.

In 1989, the new stadium in Sandy Ground was dedicated to the memory of Alberic A. Richards.[7]

---

[7] Compiled by Alex Reiph.

Owning succession land or indivdual property, and one's own house is a core socio-cultural value of the St. Martin character. Etching: "The Artist's House," by Roland Richardson.

One of the Virgin Islands' outstanding social and political activists during the first half of the twentieth century was *Marie Richards*. A 1925 registered nurse graduate, and contemporary of the great Cruzan freedom fighter, David Hamilton Jackson, Richards wrote poetry, sang and recorded kaiso, and played the guitar. She influenced the labor, political, and universal suffrage movements as a civic leader and editorial writer for *The Herald* newspaper. According to her godson, Clarence "Cherra" Heyliger, Richards was proud of her St. Martin roots. She constantly expressed love for the island of her birth and a brother she left there. A busy professional and public life did not keep this life-long philanthropist from regularly writing plays and producing cultural shows for her church.

1893(?)-1960

In Evelyn Richardson's *Seven Streets by Seven Streets*, a book about the town of Frederiksted, the life and works of the dynamic St. Martin woman comes alive: "The late Marie Richards, R. N., a native of St. Martin, lived in the United States for many years, became a citizen, and died ... in St. Croix. During her years in the Virgin Islands, she was very active in education, health, and politics. She wrote poetry and calypso songs and played the guitar. After graduating from the Frederiksted Municipal Hospital during the Naval Administration, she worked as a Public Health nurse for the Red Cross until stricken in later years by glaucoma. Some of the tunes she composed such as 'Doan Tie Yo Donkey Dung Here,' 'Keep From Roger Bridge,' 'Okra, Fungi, and Fish,' and others were recorded. On the political side, she was a Democrat and one of the signers of the franchise permitting women in the Virgin Islands to vote. ... Marie Richards was a devout Roman Catholic, involved in all of the church's activities. She also played an active role in civic affairs during the struggle between David Hamilton Jackson and the sugar plantation owners that led to the strike of field laborers in 1915. Though not on the staff of their newspaper, *The Herald*, she wrote many of the editorials. She was a fighter for human rights and Frederiksted lost a great personage when she passed on."

In his study of outstanding Virgin Islanders, Eddie Bobo portrays Richards through the words of her contemporaries as "A natural and prolific writer; warm, and concerned ... with the audacity of a Ruby Rouse and the compassion of a nurse." To

Heyliger, "As a civic leader, V. I. history must rank her among the best. ... She was instrumental in securing the right of women to vote. With the late Frederick Dorsch, Marie Richards made some really big political moves which benefitted the masses of the people here in the 1930's."

During the 1940s, Richards read her poem "Man, My Brother" over a Voice of America broadcast in honor of the World War II-bound Virgin Islands soldiers—drafted into US military service for the first time. A founding member of the Democrat Party in St. Croix, and "linked with the early formation and operations of the St. Croix labor union," Richards was also considered "a cultural bearer." Though blind in latter years, she continued to speak her mind on issues and appeared on radio programs with her guitar, promoting stringband music.

Marie Richards excelled in her professional and community responsibilities in her new island-home. Her fine human and leadership qualities represented the best of St. Martin's culture. Richards contributed in concrete and exemplary ways to the evolving and progressive principles and activities that are needed to keep forwarding a working and successful Caribbean Nationhood.

St. Martiners abroad have been known for involving themselves in positive activities. Above, St. Martiners and a few Caribbean friends dressed for a costume party in Aruba at the "St. Martin Club." Source: Harold Arnell, circa late 1940s-early 1950s.

1917-1988

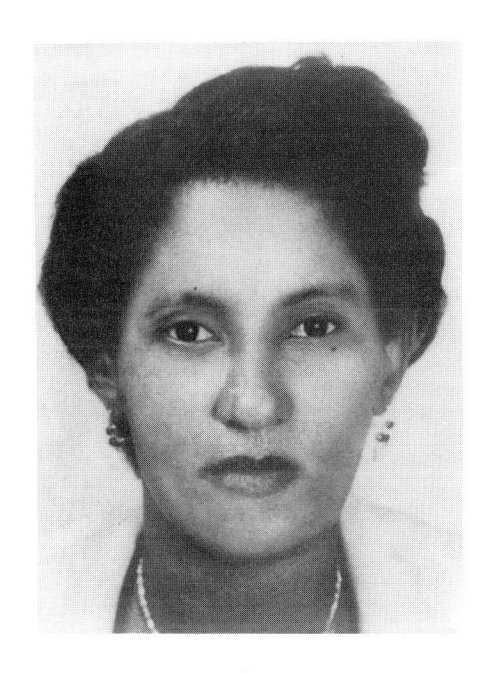

𝓛eonides Richardson was a political activist and opinion leader. Richardson was a long-time fighter for the rights of St. Martiners through her tested alliances with political people such as José Lake, Sr., Jas Bryant-Labega, Piasco Wilson, Hugh Lopes, and Wallace Peterson. During elections, she organized "contact meetings" at her home. At campaign rallies this grass roots politician fearlessly spoke against government corruption and victimization.

Richardson, affectionately called "Bahba," encouraged the people to work together for a better St. Martin. She believed in and worked openly and selflessly for democracy and accountable government, at great risk and suffering to herself and her children. At times, remembered businessman Raphael Friday, "Bahba" and her young children were the only people visible at the Oranje School meeting area for José Lake's political speeches. Scores of other people would be hiding beyond the lighted area, peering through the dark of night, through the windows, listening in silence to Lake.

Richardson's "Downstreet" home was a hearth for neighborhood children. Many heeded her advice on the need to be what she called, "independent in yourself" to succeed professionally and as human beings. Richardson and her ten children were often taunted, called "wara-wara," and told to get "outta Town" because of her political affiliations. (The wara-wara is a bird of prey whose range includes Curacao and is family to the killy-killy found in St. Martin.) This independent-thinking woman's affiliations aligned her against the Democratic Party "machine" of Claude Wathey and his supporters.

In a posthumous tribute, political leader Vance James, Jr., recalled Richardson as a giant who was "... among the first women to be active in politics on this island. She did not, as so many, choose the safe side, instead she chose the side of what she considered to be right, and she fought the fight for justice against the establishment. She was never known to be a candidate for office, but she was an activist campaigning and speaking out against all odds. Bahba did not feel that because she was getting help for her children this meant she had to be quiet about the things she believed in. And because of her conviction and her outspokenness, her home was where the political motorcades of the day would stop and make lots of noise and the slogans of 'out of Town' and 'wara-wara' were hurled at her."

The persecution of Richardson and her family reached a critical point when, because of her activism, her children could find no work in St. Martin. One political boss declared at a 1960s election rally that "No Friday will find work in St. Martin!" (Friday and Richardson are the last names of Richardson's children.) The single mother, then in her forties, migrated to the United States of America to support her family. By working and simultaneously completing studies in computer operations, this hard-working St. Martin woman continued to set an example for her children of what it meant to be "independent in yourself." She also took courses in political science.

Leonides Richardson's legacy is a great inspiration to her family. A number of her sons returned to St. Martin and became businessmen, founding members of political parties and business associations, and public opinion leaders.

*L*ionel B. Scott was a builder, businessman, and politician. He was born in St. Martin on January 28, 1897, into a large, poor family. The industrious Scott built himself into a worldly, respectable, and wealthy man by the time of his death in 1966. After his early schooling in Great Bay, a young L. B. Scott emigrated to the Dominican Republic where he worked on sugarcane estates. He eventually took up vocational study and work in construction.

Between 1914 and 1930, the Dominican Republic was a Caribbean boom town which attracted many immigrant laborers. It was also a hotbed of political and social activism. The immigrants were mostly contract field workers, some factory and dock workers, English-speaking, and from throughout the Caribbean. Most of the Caribbean peoples were under the yoke of European colonialism.

The political and social ideology of the day which rallied the dispossessed Black masses worldwide was Garveyism. The organization which articulated forcefully the inalienable need and profound steps necessary for the Black man's salvation was the Universal Negro Improvement Association (UNIA). Maybe it was because of their egalitarian village culture, the spirit of independence which self-reliance breeds, the confidence of being comparatively landed, or their aptitude for languages, but the St. Martiners, such as James Cooks and Thomas Duruo, managed to emerge as key leaders and driving UNIA forces in the Spanish-speaking country. Scott stepped right into the thick of things like Compa Nansi in the Brer patch.

In a 1961 *Windward Islands Opinion*, we read that Scott "... was active in the 'Garvey Movement'" and a past UNIA chapter president. Scott returned to his beloved St. Martin in 1929, "... to use his knowledge and experience for the benefit of his beloved St. Maarten and her people.

"In the beginning it was very rough because the older folks were not willing to listen ... to this 'upstart boy' *(as they termed him)*." Scott became a founding member and first president of the Philipsburg Mutual Improvement Association (PMIA) in 1933. Patterned after the UNIA, PMIA was a benevolent or civic association formed to improve men and women for leadership, based on self-reliance in social, cultural, economic, and political fields.

It was in the construction field, however, where "Brother Bo," as he was well known, proved to be meritorious and earned his wealth. Among the testimonies to Scott's ability as a builder and contractor are the Methodist Mission House in Great Bay (Philipsburg), Mount William Hill Road; the Harbor Building and former Administration Building in Saba; and the Administrator's House and "government school" in St. Eustatius. As government contractor for the Windward Islands, he directed the construction of the early airstrip in Simpson Bay which later became the busy Princess Juliana International Airport. This early nation builder served as foreman for the Windward Islands Public Works Department for over twenty-two years until he resigned in 1952. By 1961, he was the Esso gasoline dealer. (The Scott family operated the gasoline station until it was destroyed by Hurricane Luis on September 5, 1995.)

A better-than-average financial standing allowed Scott to turn his attention to active politics. In 1937, he was "elected" to the Court of Policy *(Raad van Politie)*, a two-member body empowered by a limited electorate to advise the lieutenant governor, then Johan Diderich Meiners, on local matters. During his thirteen years as a *"Landsraad,"* or "National Councilor," Scott was a passionate opponent of government centralization in Willemstad, Curacao. He argued with political contemporaries that centralization led to the neglect of St. Martin (South), Saba, St. Eustatius, Aruba, and Bonaire.

No doubt a result of the Round Table Conferences which began in 1946 between the "Dutch Antilles" and colonial Holland, an early form of Islands Regulations *(Eilandenregeling)* went into effect on March 14, 1951. The new regulations allowed limited internal "administration" for the Dutch colonies in the Caribbean. In 1951, L. B. Scott ran for political office as a candidate of the Nationale Volkspartij (NVP)[8] "chapter" in St. Martin—headed by a 24-year-old Claude A. Wathey. Scott was elected one of NVP's four councilors in the five-member Island Council. Melford Hazel was the opposition Democratic Party's (DP) sole councilor. Then came the 1955 election. Political parties changed "colors." Wathey became leader of the DP and won the election. "Brother Bo" remained with NVP which was now headed by Hazel. Scott at one time served as president of St. Martin's NVP "chapter." Incidentally, the Curacao-based NVP was founded in 1949 by the illustrious Dr. Moises Frumencio da Costa Gomez. Dr. da Costa Gomez was a principal developer of the 1954 *Statuut* which granted The Netherlands Antilles autonomy within the colonial Dutch Kingdom.

In 1959, Scott led NVP and was elected as the opposition leader in the Island Council. The last Island Council election Scott contested was in 1963. He was again elected to the opposition seat but not without controversy. NVP candidate José Lake, Sr., received the party's highest amount of votes, but Scott was seated instead. By the time of his death in office, "Brother Bo" the public servant, had gained "for himself a reputation especially for his readiness of speech and the honest and skillful way in which he was watchful of the people's interest," stated a Postal Service brochure in 1974. That same year, the Postal Service issued a stamp bearing the old battler's image.

No reference to "Brother Bo" is complete without mentioning his love for horses which made him known throughout the Caribbean of his day. There are tales of dramatic horse races between the Scotts' men and horse-raising families in the North. Reporter Lloyd Richardson wrote that these races, in which L. B. Scott's favorite dark brown stallions, "Duke" and "Piensamente," took part, were held in Marigot Hill—probably on the hilly road which straddles the border between the South and North. Scott was a tall man with the striking features of an ancient African warrior chief. He was reputedly a handsome sight on horseback when wearing his wide-brim cowboy hat and knee-high black boots. An equestrian breeder who took great pleasure in the fruits of the land, and himself owner of an estate of former slave masters, Scott believed that St. Martin's development should be linked to agriculture and animal husbandry.

Scott is also remembered as having aristocratic bearing and for being a disciplinarian. The latter aspect is the source of some unfavorable rumors about Scott which have persisted among the St. Martin population long after his death.

In a 1955 letter to his son, he wrote: "There is no success without sacrifice." However ambiguous the personality traits of men and women may be viewed during their lifetime or after their passing, Will Johnson reminded us in *For The Love of St. Maarten*, that "Mr. Scott had a human quality about him which endeared him to all who came in contact with him."

Before his death, Lionel Bernard Scott was awarded the gold medal of the Order of Oranje-Nassau by the Dutch Queen. A posthumous tribute was paid to this dynamic son-of-the-soil when the government in Great Bay named the main road into Cul-de-sac (South) in his honor.

---

[8] *Founded in Curacao in 1949, by the illustrious Dr. M. F. da Costa Gomez, the NVP officially changed its name in 1982 to Partido Nashonal di Pueblo (People's National Party).*

Horses at St. John's ranch. Etching: "At St. John's," by Roland Richardson.

S*imeone* **Venter-Trott** was an early educator, seamstress, and photographer. She is best remembered as a pre-school teacher and catechist. Venter-Trott hailed from Concordia and had a profound influence on the social development and religious upbringing of a number of St. Martin's children.

Historian Daniella Jeffry eulogized Venter-Trott as "an extraordinary lady" whose "great concern for children urged her to open a school in 1941. She took charge not only of their academic education but also of their religious and moral education." In the 1940s, this community organizer served as a nurse's aid to the outspoken doctor Pitat from Guadeloupe. (Dr. Pitat had a medical practice in Marigot.) With her aptitude for the French language, and armed with her *Certificat d'Etudes*, the highest education degree obtainable on the island during the first half of the twentieth century, "Miss Sissie" or "Ma'zelle Sissie," as Venter-Trott was affectionately and respectfully called, was a trusted reader of French language documents for St. Martiners whose nation-tongue has historically been English.

Venter-Trott owned a shop which "sold a little of everything," including religious articles and her custom-made wedding gowns. The little shop also served as a studio where she took and developed photographs, especially for passports.

Venter-Trott became a Municipal Council member in 1959. The Municipal Council, chaired by the mayor, is the legislative branch of the elected government in the Northern part of St. Martin. In 1963, the French government awarded Simeone Venter-Trott the *Ordre National du Merite*. Following her death in 1989, the Simeone Venter-Trott Kindergarten was dedicated in Concordia. The Simeone Trott Impasse is located in The Spring.

1908–1989

1918 — 1994

*P*aul Antonin Whit, Sr., rose from humble beginnings to become a leading political party founder and one of St. Martin's enduring businessmen.

Whit (pronounced "White") finished his basic schooling in Marigot. His father, Gillaume Albert Whit, operated a lime kiln and raised cattle in the Diamond Hill/Concordia area. Young Paul helped to tend his father's herd. The cattle were sold for breeding and for their meat. Whit's parents could not afford to send their son off-island to further his education. At the age of fifteen—two years after his mother's death—Whit started a "school" at his father's house in St. James. At his school he taught poor neighborhood children to read and write. Later on, Garveyite Nestor Bute helped Whit to conduct "classes."

As a young adult, Whit became a Marigot Prison guard. Whit eventually secured a farm plot in Sandy Ground. From Low Town he would row his small boat across the northern reaches of Simpson Bay Lagoon to work his "grounds." On weekends he sold fruit and provisions at Marigot Market. The young farmer's always bountiful crop of sweet potatoes and pigeon peas was much sought after from Marigot to Great Bay during the Christmas season. The industrious Whit also sold the fish he caught in the fertile lagoon. (During this time some St. Martiners considered the then plentiful lobster not a delicacy but "hog food.")

Savings from farming, fishing, and selling clothes from his house, helped Whit to buy a motor for his boat and to open a clothing store along with his wife, Theodorine, in the late 1950s.

In 1956, the first of the Whits' seven children was born (the couple also adopted the children of a deceased relative). Whit's business endeavors and family responsibilities did not prevent his political involvement.

Before the age of thirty, his public life had begun. By the mid-1940s, he found a trusted friend in another hard-working, conscientious young man, Felix Choisy. Though from different socio-economic backgrounds, Choisy, the manager of his father's estate, and the self-made Whit loved St. Martin and her people dearly. Both sons-of-the-soil were influenced by the Garveyite teachings of Thomas Emmanuel Duruo up in Rambaud; the Negritude Movement sweeping out of Paris into France's African and Caribbean colonies; the workers' rights struggles sweeping the globe; the spirit of emancipation that swept the island in 1848; and the universal principles popularized in the West by the French Revolution—*Liberté, Egalité, Fraternité*.

Choisy and Whit were principal founders of Le Rassemblement Democratique. The political party became the vocal and dauntless opponent of then Mayor Louis Constant Fleming and his administration. Whit was branded an upstart, a militant, and a communist by the political establishment.

In 1947, Whit and Choisy founded *Esprit De La Jeunesse (Spirit of Youth)*. According to Whit, the four-page English/French newspaper was the political, economic, and social news organ of Le Rassemblement Democratique. St. Martiners from both sides of the island read and advertised in *Spirit of Youth*. Those who dared to publicly support the paper included Simon Jeffry, Ph. Richardson, Oswald Rohan, Leon Chance, and A. Halley. Whit was the newspaper's political director and director of publication.

Forty-seven years after *Spirit of Youth* was first published, Whit was described in his eulogy as: "... A quiet, perhaps overly modest man, acutely conscious of his responsibilities. He was a man of high standard, complete integrity, and boundless enthusiasm for whatever task he took in hand. ... What he preached he practiced. ... He fought hard for every cause in which he enlisted, and the causes for which he fought were right and just."

Whit's cause, as reflected in the *Spirit of Youth* during its two years of publication, was the upliftment of the consciousness and living standards of St. Martin's people. He saw the paper as dedicated, in Choisy's words, to the "glory of St. Martin ... at the head of emancipation, messenger of truth, freedom, and justice. ..." Whit spoke out bravely, wrote with foresight, and organized from the grass roots against the illiteracy, mis-education, economic exploitation, racism, and political victimization during the last three decades of Traditional St. Martin. Some claim that this St. Martin man was singularly crucial in breaking up the decades-old Fleming monopoly in the Northern part of the island. What is certain is Whit's consistent leadership role in the social, political, and economic transformation to modern St. Martin.

During the 1940s, he was one of the organizers of what might have been the first Labor Day march on the island. The gentle giant has been described as a bedrock of principles "at the root of the political activism that issued in the administration of former Mayor Hubert Petit. ..." From 1959 to 1978, Whit served as a Commune Councilman in the Petit administration. In a 1994 *Newsday* article, Whit was hailed as "A true St. Martin patriot."

The political administrations Whit battled publicly during the 1940s and 1950s were unable to "squeeze" him out of the picture as one reportedly threatened to do in an October 1947 "conference ... dedicated to the *Spirit of Youth*." He was able to find a balance between his political activism and responsibilities as a husband, father, and businessman. In 1977, Whit expanded his business by opening the Paul Whit & Brothers Furniture Store in St. James. Like his contemporary Melford Hazel, Whit's pioneering examples in business and socio-political activism inspired his family tremendously. (Whit's sons Paul and Horace and adopted sons Adrian and Alain Richardson are businessmen. Horace and Alain are leading political activists and principals of St. Martin Educational & Cultural Organization. The Whits' children founded the Soualiga supermarket.)

In 1988, Paul A. Whit, Sr., was a recipient of SMECO's Certificate of Excellence for his work in politics during the 1940s and 1950s. In 1994, Whit received the Commune Father's Day Award for Leadership and Responsibility in the Home and Community.

Chapter 3

The Nature Of St. Martin

pass you by

like every living organism

years grow older

finally, I heard you cry

        but softly

once sun shone upon you

once full moon made love over you

banklakes purified by salt

but you were sweet.

— Esther Gumbs,

Salt Pond

PONDS OF ST. MARTIN

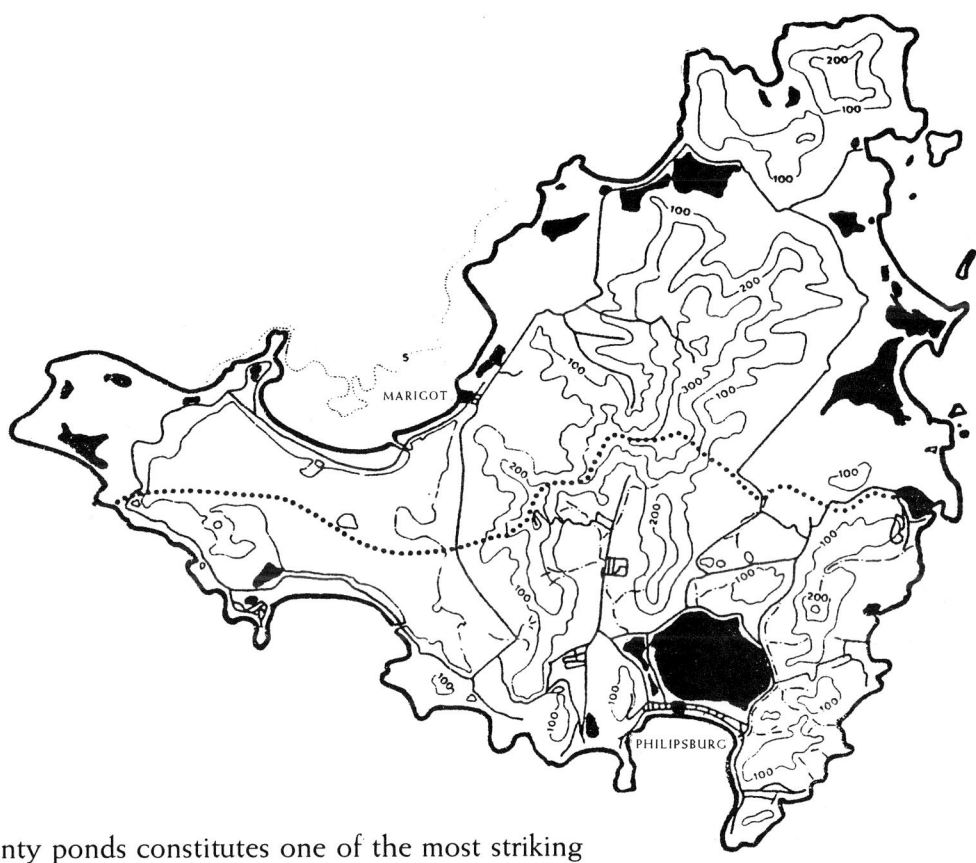

A ring of over twenty ponds constitutes one of the most striking natural features of St. Martin. Stringed along Lowlands, and between the shores and the bottom of our many hills, the fresh and salt water ponds are essential for the balanced survival of an ecosystem which includes human, animal, and plant life, reefs, bays, beaches, wetlands, and uplands.

St. Martin's inland ponds, with mostly brackish water, serve as nature's barriers between the hills and beaches by catching most of the mud and silt-laden rain water running down from the hills. In the more built up and deforested areas and badly excavated hillsides, "mud rivers" rush down and empty into the ponds. Sewage is pumped into some ponds. Were it not for these natural catchments, mud and silt would reach the beaches and (a) cause the destruction of coral and other marine life, affect gradual current shifts in some areas and beach erosion, and pollute the coastal sea; (b) adversely affect the livelihood of fishermen; and (c) make the white, and in some areas pink, fine-grain sandy beaches coarse

GREAT SALT POND
FRESH POND
LITTLE BAY POND
MULLET BAY POND
FLAMINGO POND
LOWLANDS PONDS
RED POND
MARIGOT POND
FRIAR'S BAY POND
GRAND CASE SALT POND
FISH POND
ORIENT SALT POND
CHEVRISE POND
OYSTER POND
GUANA BAY POND

with dirt, rock, and wood fragments and broken glass. Beaches that are uncomfortable, rough, unsafe, or unattractive to St. Martin's "weekend" sea-bath aficionados, picnicking families, and beach-loving vacationers would have negative and wide-ranging environmental effects, disastrous consequences for the tourism-oriented economy, and limit recreational possibilities for our people.

From about 1631, the ponds of Sualouiga have been besieged by man, and these environmental basins are now in need of cleaning and protection. The first Europeans to exploit the island's salt resources, though minimally, were the Spaniards. The wide-scale exploitation of the salt ponds, especially the Great Salt Pond, started with the Dutch, followed by the French. Salt was "picked" from the Great Salt Pond, and the salt ponds of Grand Case, Orleans, Chevrise, and Lowlands (Red Bay). The vital commodity and food preservative literally "fueled" long-distance trade.

The last serious salt-picking from the Great Salt Pond's "pans" occurred in the 1920s. Salt-picking continued as a faltering industry up to the 1940s. Salt picked in Grand Case during the 1960s was economically insignificant. At the time of this writing, the 1983 observation of the parks foundation, STINAPA-Sint Maarten, holds true: "In Sint Maarten we can see many examples of unwise and thoughtless usage of the ponds. Dumping and piping in of sewage, waste material, and oil; the cleaning of cement, dump, and septic trucks; and the clearing of the shore vegetation" damage our island's beautiful scenery and destroy plant and animal life in and around the ponds.

The Great Salt Pond

The most prominent and historic of St. Martin's ponds is the Great Salt Pond. Up to the early decades of the twentieth century, the great pond was recorded as measuring "1 square mile in area, and almost circular in shape." Since 1966, over 200 meters of the Great Salt Pond have been filled with dirt. The dirt was carted to the "Pondfill" by trucks, especially from Fort Hill (leaving a gaping deforested scar on the hill's eastern face). The continuing "pond filling" accommodates the expanding city of Great Bay (Philipsburg). In a 1973 *Windward Islands Opinion* editorial, the late crusading newspaperman José Lake, Sr., likened the careless urban development and wanton filling of the great pond by government to "a pig's pen" instead of "the extension and enlargement of

Town." The main garbage dump for Southern St. Martin is located on a peninsula of the landfill that juts into the heart of the once bountiful, salt-producing pond. The volume of garbage increases daily. With the help of an occasional tractor which levels the piles of refuse, the dump heap spreads like a menacing barge toward Sucker Garden's "Pondside." In 1996, the Great Salt Pond measured 185.1 hectares.

Public outcry against pond pollution, unplanned building, and unrestricted land-filling continues. The dedicated activists of St. Maarten National Heritage Foundation, formerly STINAPA-Sint Maarten, and other environmentally-conscious persons have written in newspapers, spoken on radio and television programs, and filed their concerns for pond clean-up and conservation with government authorities. The island's media have called attention to the periodic stench emitted from the Great Salt Pond and the offensive and unhealthy smoke that drifts over the city when the garbage is set on fire. There have been calls for the construction of a pollution-regulating recycling plant at a new dump site.

The Great Salt Pond and landfill area should be cleaned, zoned, and the parameters converted into a tree-lined park with proper lighting and telecommunications and sanitary facilities. The park should include lanes for joggers, cyclists, and pedestrians. At least two small amphitheaters for outdoor concerts, dramatic performances, and other cultural exhibitions could be built. Attractively designed vending stalls, for the preparation and sale of St. Martin/Caribbean cultural goods and foods could become a main attraction for such a circular park. The highly successful 1993, 1994, 1995, and 1996 Carnival Jouvert around the Great Salt Pond indicate how such a "parkway" would benefit the nation's culture, recreational infrastructure, and tourism image. A salt crystal miniature festival is possible when the salt is ripe or "blowing."

An impressive, albeit controversial proposal, to clean, "develop," and zone the Great Salt Pond was prepared in 1990 by Louis Crastell Gumbs. The proposal of the then novice St. Martin Minister of Transport & Communications included building on the current landfill an environment-friendly, spacious resort city within a city—complete with a fine arts complex, museum, national library, public park, and a golf course to cover up the garbage dump. The plan did not get beyond the dossier Gumbs presented to the government in Great Bay.

SALT HARVESTING, GRAND CASE

A historical overview

The salt-pans of Great Bay, Grand Case, Orleans, Chevrise, and to a lesser extent, Baie Rouge, were for St. Martin what the sugar-cane, tobacco, and cotton plantations were for most of the Caribbean and the Americas during the brutal centuries of slavery. Exploitation of salt ponds and the Black people who slaved and worked in their briny waters by the emerging mercantile powers of post-Columbian Europe can be placed within the context of the beginnings of modern world trade.

In a 1990 study of St. Martin's Fort Amsterdam, engineer Diederik Six related the rise of Holland's international trade to the exploitation of salt. Following the end of the eighty-year war with Spain in the early seventeenth century, Holland started to build up her naval power. The Dutch East India Company (1602-1798) was chartered by the Dutch government, and the Dutch West Indies Company was established. "The West Indies trade company concentrated (*its*) interests in the Europe-Africa-America triangle. Boats from Holland sailed to West Africa with yellow bricks, guns, cloth, and geneva on board. On the Gold Coast, the ships were loaded with gold, ivory, salt, and fish. Another important trade was the slave trade. The slaves were transported to Brazil where they were put to work in the sugar mills. Gold, sugar, salt, tobacco, tortoise shell, and the African products were shipped back to Holland. The tortoise shell was used to make picture frames and small exclusive items.

"Salt is very important to protect food against going bad. The high concentration of salt in the sea water, the good temperature, and the natural basins make St. Maarten a favorite salt spot. 'The island contained three large salt basins capable of supplying more than four hundred boat-loads of salt a year.' The strategic situation and the interesting salt quantities were of common interest for the Dutch traders and the Spanish conquerors, thus conflicts were unavoidable."

"Salt and salt ponds[9]

"Salt Ponds are scattered almost all over the island. The Great Salt Pond is 1 sq. mile in area, and almost circular in shape. It lies directly at the foot of the hills which surround it on the sides. To avoid the rain water caught on these hills flowing into it, a proper system of drainage was constructed by Dutch engineers.

"A dyke or 'ring-dam' built on the northern side dams off from 100 to 300 ft. of the pond from the main body of water. The drainage from the northern hills flows into this dammed-off portion which in like manner delivers the accumulated water to two canals, one on the eastern and one on the western side. They convey the drainage to the sea. The canal on the eastern side is called Roland's Canal, from its constructor; the one on the western side flows from an accumulator or collector, the Fresh Pond, to the sea and bears the name of Trench. The pond is also divided into larger and smaller concessions by dams.

"The history of salt ponds and salt industry is a lengthy affair; however, I shall try to condense certain things of interest. ...

"Prior to 1858, the Great Salt Pond belonged to the public who derived such benefits from it as their means would allow; the Treaty of Concordia on March 23rd, 1648, provided for such. ...

"On June 27th of 1858, was granted to Mr. Perinnon, a former Governor of Martinique, the right to establish for his benefit such works on the portion of pond, situated behind ... Philipsburg.

"He was allowed to exploit this pond, and obliged to pay a royalty of 5 cents (Dutch) on each barrel reaped on a production of 100,000. He was also allowed to occupy the lands bordering the northern side of the pond—the Madams Estate. The lease was granted for 80 years. After having exhausted his capital on drainage systems for the ponds, Mr. Perinnon relinquished the lease ... before completion of the works, to the Saline Exploitation Co. (Exploitatie Maatschappij van Zoutmeren) *(which)*, represented by Messrs. Gordon and Van Stolk, *(was)* to complete the works with the understanding that a certain percent of all expenditure made by their Co. would come to *(it)*, and after recovery of the capital expended on works and exploitation, the ponds would return to Perinnon. In order to retain the ponds, the Saline Co. made sure not to recover the extended capital. When, however, the Co. found that the amount of salt marketed did not bring enough interest to cover the expense of pond upkeep (they kept the ponds in good condition), they too sought their abandonment. The high-salaried director was soon recalled, and later on, the sub-director discontinued.

"In 1907, Messrs. L. A. van Romondt's Sons of the Netherlands Part bought out the Exploitatie-Maatschappij's share for fl. 25,000 into whose hands the greater portions of the pond have remained till today. Smaller concessionaires (private parties) own smaller damned-off portions of the pond, the former St. Martin Co. concessions (...), today represented by Messrs. D. C. van Romondt & Co. and L. A. van Romondt's Sons.

"The Salt industry of St. Martin has almost breathed its last, an industry on which 'St. Maarten' was wholly and solely dependent. In spite of the modern age of speed and machinery—presumably too on account of lack of capital—the same old-time methods are not only employed, but expediencies for hastening salt production have been allowed to fall to ruin, such as: windmills for pumping off the perpendicular rainfall, dykes and dams which divided the pond's surface into smaller portions for speeding up evaporation and crystal formation by allowing less ripple and causing more stagnancy. It would take hundreds of thousands of guilders to rebuild these necessary factors. ...

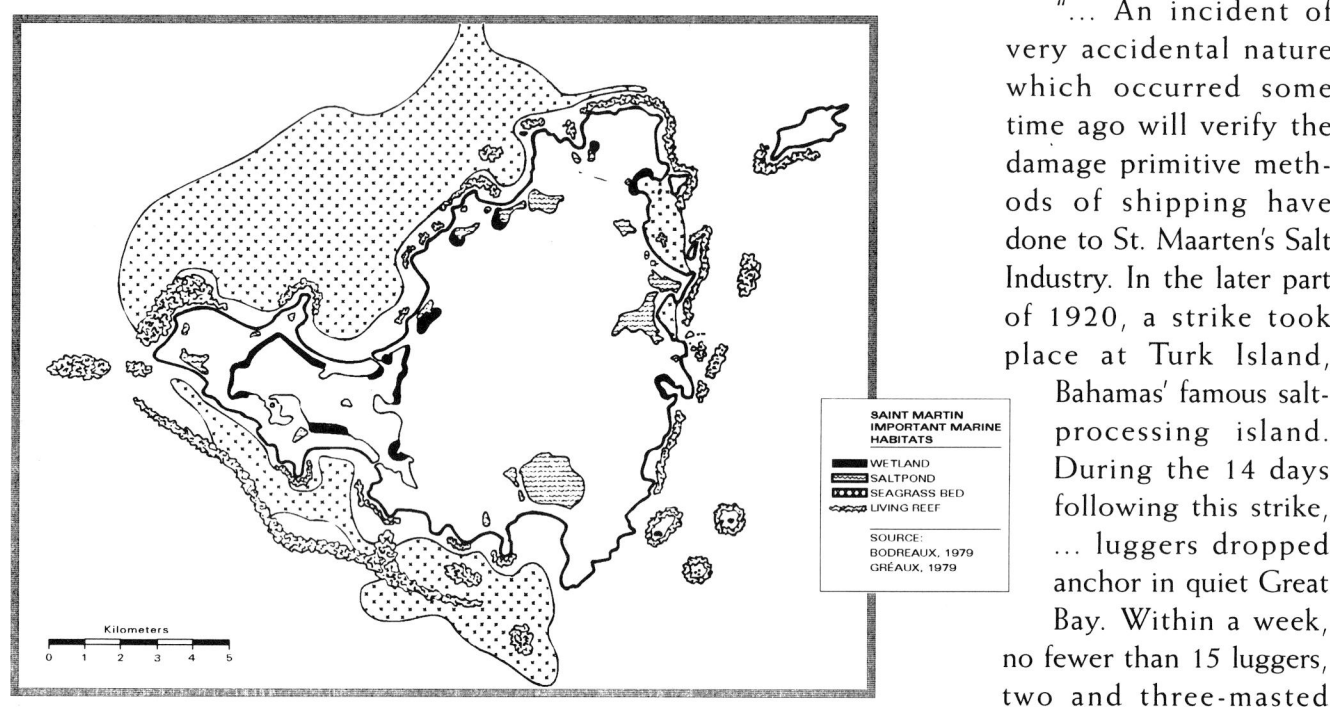

"... An incident of very accidental nature which occurred some time ago will verify the damage primitive methods of shipping have done to St. Maarten's Salt Industry. In the later part of 1920, a strike took place at Turk Island, Bahamas' famous salt-processing island. During the 14 days following this strike, ... luggers dropped anchor in quiet Great Bay. Within a week, no fewer than 15 luggers, two and three-masted schooners, lay at anchor awaiting their briny cargo. Unfortunately, some of them called for fine or 'ground salt,' but it took whole 7 days for a small toy-like crusher and gasoline motor to crush sufficient natrium chloride in order to supply the 3000-barrel wants of the first lugger. The 15th drogher, unwilling to wait her turn after three months, quietly set sail, and accompanied by others which soon followed suit, many staunch droghers quietly departed to the sorrow of the labouring class.

"Much ado has been made about market, but experience has taught that a market can always be found for a good article, and St. Maarten's salt rivals with the world's best. A step into Mr. C. Wathey's Office, former Offices of Messrs. L. A. V. R's Sons will confirm this statement; a 'Diplome de Grand Prix' awarded Messrs. L. A. V. R.'s Sons, for the best product, by the 'Exposition Universelle Bruxelles 1910' hangs in above-mentioned office.

"A protective duty against foreign salt imported into British West Indian Islands has been somewhat of a handicap. ...

"**SALT REAPING**: As the water evaporates, tiny crystals form at the surface sink to the muddy bottom where a crystalline layer is soon formed, the growth of which depends largely on the heat of the weather and speed of evaporation. The best quality salt is formed in 72 cm. (about 28 in.) deep water. When the crystalline mass has reached the thickness from 2 to 4 inches, 'reapers' enter the briny water and break up the crust with iron or wooden rods. It is then thrown into baskets and washed until the desired quality is reached. The reapers dump the cleaned product into square flat-bottomed boats, 'flats.' The flats bear the load of white glistening crystals shorewards where it is piled in heaps, 'salt heaps.'

"During the time of 'blowing,' after complete saturation of the body of water, the pond puts on violet and pink hues. ... The ponds are then very beautiful, especially when seen from the neighbouring heights.

"Miniature ships, and other novelties rigged up of thread and other material, are placed in the pond during the blowing season by novelty fans. After from 24 hours to 2 days, according to the strength of the brine—they are withdrawn from the pond 'crystal-laden.' They resemble icicle-covered ships or ships after a snow storm. The superfluous crystal can be reduced with hot water. After standing in the sun two or three hours, the miniatures become real novelties worth possessing.

"During crystallization, projecting portions of sticks and branches lying near the shore become entirely covered with glittering crystals, hence the idea of misinformed strangers that salt 'grows' in the pond."

Report on the Great Salt Pond in 1839 and an account of salt-picking in 1789

"The earliest document which we *(Abraham Cannegieter and Richard*

PRODUCTION DES ETANGS

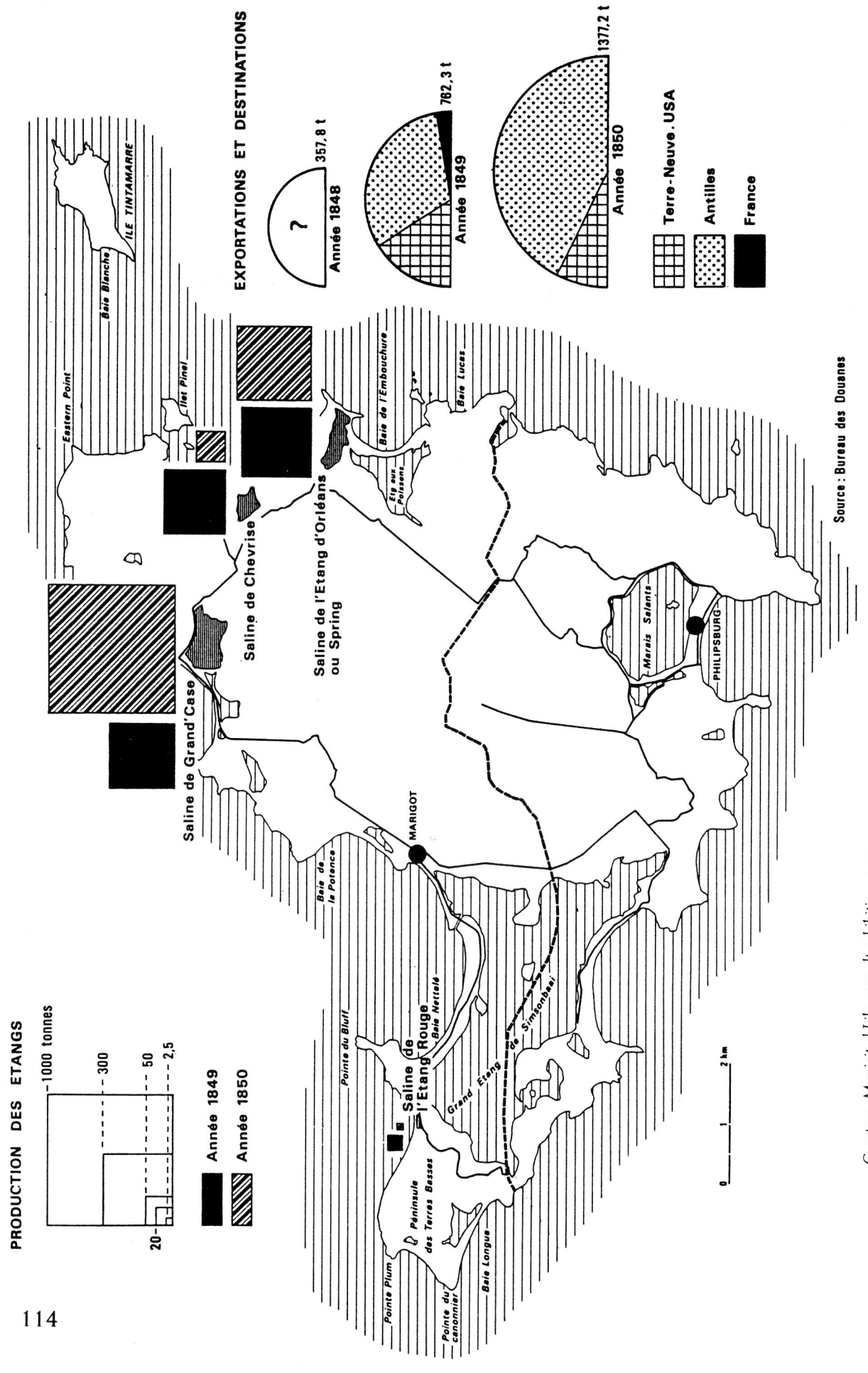

- 1000 tonnes
- 300
- 50
- 20
- 2,5

Année 1849
Année 1850

EXPORTATIONS ET DESTINATIONS

Année 1848 — 357,8 t
Année 1849 — 762,3 t
Année 1850 — 1377,2 t

Terre-Neuve. USA
Antilles
France

Source: Bureau des Douanes

Saline de Grand'Case
Saline de Chevrise
Saline de l'Etang d'Orléans ou Spring
Saline de l'Etang Rouge

ILE TINTAMARRE
Baie Blanche
Eastern Point
Ilet Pinel
Baie de l'Embouchure
Etg aux Poissons
Baie Lucas
Marais Salants
PHILIPSBURG
MARIGOT
Baie de la Potence
Pointe du Bluff
Baie Nettelé
Péninsule des Terres Basses
Pointe Plum
Pointe du canonnier
Baie Longue
Grand Etang de Simsonbaai

Courtesy: Municipal Library salt exhibition, 1995.

114

Robinson Richardson) found among the archives of this colony relative to the salt pond in the Dutch part of St. Martin is a petition, dated the 28 August 1778 signed by 162 of the principal inhabitants of the Dutch part of St. Martin, to the West India Company in Holland, against an offer which it seems had been made by a Mr. Henricus Godet of this island, to purchase, or lease the said salt pond from the said West India Company.

"That we have not been able to discover any other important document relative to the salt pond in this colony, nor the treaty of 1648, is not however the least astonishing, because in the year 1810 when the British captured this island, ... their military force marched into ... Philipsburg, and occupied the Court House ... as a barrack. In the Secretary's Office in that building was deposited all the archives of the colony, and the day after their occupation, ... the said Secretary Office had been broken open, the papers and books taken from the desk and shelves, and thrown on the floor, a great many of the papers torn in pieces, and rendered useless, and the whole cast in utter confusion. ... (It) is more than probable, that if the treaty of 1648 had been among the archives, that it was then destroyed. ...

"Experience proved that until the pond water weighed 10 dutch pounds per gallon, the pond did not commence 'to blow,' which is the local phrase, and signifies the beginning to make salt.

"Before this period the pond water has been drying out from the heat of the sun which has varied little from 90 to 92 degrees of Fahrenheit thermometer in the shade and out of it 108 to 110 degrees. ... The pond water ... then begins to boil into salt by the same action and heat, and during the day, the surface of the pond, from the weight of the water, has not a ripple on it, but resembles a large mirror, it is crusted over with an extremely thin cake of salt, about half the thickness of a barley corn, during the whole of the heat of the day the crust of salt is thickening, as the shades of evening come on, and of course the water becomes cooler, this crust of salt sinks to the bottom and there remains; from day to day this process goes on, and as each crust daily goes down, they heap one upon the other, undergo, a coaction, and after five or six weeks from the commencement of the blowing of the pond, ... the salt is formed into beautiful chrystalizations, and into cakes of about an inch square, it is then ripe, and fit for reaping, weighing 96 pounds Dutch per bushel.

"As soon as the pond begins 'to blow' an order was issued

by the Governor, to forbid persons from crossing over it, in boats or flats, and competent persons were appointed, to report to the Governor, the Progressive State of the salt. As soon as it was understood to be certain that a crop of salt might be expected to be reaped, public notice was given by the Governor to all the inhabitants of the island, without mentioning either Dutch or French, ...

"The opening of the pond, in the first day of reaping salt in the Year 1789 ... (t)he whole length of the southern shore, nearly one mile, was crowded with inhabitants of both, which could not have been less in number that six or seven thousand persons, five hundred flats stood ready, with their laborers alongside them so that at the given signal, each flat had some fanciful flag and the negro women, who were laborers in them, had their many colored handkerchiefs fixed to small poles, and waved them in the air. ...

"The salt pond before, was beautifully white with salt and promised a glorious crop, and the sun having risen in all his glory, as though he claimed the torrid zone for his exclusive empire, was the moment for the signal gun to be fired from the fort, announcing that the pond might be entered, the shouts of the whole assemblage greeted the intelligence, and each flat pushed off, eager to be the first to load and to return, and throw a basket of salt on the pond side, when to receive a small customary reward which was more value as the triumph of superior industry, than from any other motive; some idea may be formed of the great value of a salt crop in this island, by considering the size of the flats employed, which vary from 15 to 25 feet long, and from 8 to 12 feet wide, they are perfectly flat bottomed, and made of the lightest wood, so that when filled with salt, carrying from 25 to 40 barrels each flat, they do not require more than eight inches of water to float them. From 12 to 15 laborers, men and women are required to one flat, and each laborer is reckoned to pick ten barrels of salt per day.

"**THE MANNER OF PICKING IS THUS:** The flat being steadily moored in about two feet of water, and never more than three, which is the deepest part of the pond when in a state for reaping of salt; each laborer belonging to the flat is provided with a small wicker basket, whose reticulations are sufficiently large to permit the water to pass speedily through it. He then commences his work, putting the basket to the bottom, and with both hands put under the cake of salt, raises up as much salt from the bottom, as he can conveniently hold, this cake is well washed in the basket, and the grains of salt thus separated, being cleaned from all extraneous matter, is thrown into the flat, which when fully laden, returns to the shore, and each owner of the salt thus reaped, makes his or her heap of salt on the allotments belonging to them, on the pond side, the heap of salt or generally built up in cones, or sometimes angular, like the roof of a house, and the salt being well pressed down, and raked, is baked together on the surface of the heap by the heat of the sun, and forms so solid a crust, that rain cannot very materially effect, or waste it, provided, that the heap has hard time to crust sufficiently. It is however commonly estimated that the loss of salt thus heaped is ten percent.

CHRONOLOGIE

LE SEL À SAINT MARTIN (1789-1961)

À la fin du XVIII siècle, la production de sel est d'environ 200.000 tonneaux de 115kg: 23.000.000kg l'an.[4]
1789 – Great Salt Pond: 3 millions de tonneaux récoltés.[2]
1792 – 750.000 tonneaux exportés.[2]
1797-1817 – Période d'arrêt.[4]
1825 – "Salt cakes" très minces.[2]
1834-1837 – Exploitations de Monsieur Gerauld de Clouz[2]
        1834 – 442 tonneaux • 1835 – 234 tonneaux
        1836 – 123 tonneaux • 1837 – 423 tonneaux.
1835 – Saint Martin Salt Company
        (27 Avril au 15 Juin): 9.895 tonneaux
        1837 – (19 Mars au 3 Mai): 4.025 tonneaux.[2]
1836 – Saint Georges Salt Company: 3.307 tonneaux
        (18 Mars au 18 Avril): 2.251 tonneaux
        (15 au 20 Novembre): 1.056 tonneaux.[2]
1836 – Union company (Octobre et Novembre): 7.182 tonneaux.[2]
1837 – General salt pond: 10.863 tonneaux
1837 – John Edney Richardson (Janvier à Mars): 595 tonneaux.[2]
1845 – Début de l'exploitation des salines de la partie Française de Saint Martin[3]
        Sel exporté par la partie Française (1848 à 1850)
        1848 – 357.805kg • 1849 – 762.300kg • 1850 – 1.377.400kg.[3]
1849 – Production Néerlandaise: 10.000.000kg de sel.[3]
1849 – Production totale des salines de la partie Française de l'île: 802.000kg
        Grand Case (Mery d'Arcy): 258.244kg • Chevrise (Mery d'Arcy): 237.393kg
        Spring ou Orléans (Beauperthuy): 291.126kg • Etang Rouge: 15.238kg.[3]
1850 – Production de la partie Néerlandaise: plus de 2 millions de tonneaux
1850 – Production de la partie Française: 1 million de tonneaux.[1]
1863 – Production totale des sel pour la partie Française: 3.600.000kg.[3]
1949 – Arrêt de la production de sel à la partie Hollandaise.[4]
1961 – Fin de l'exploitation du sel à la partie Française: la production était de 3.500 tonnes l'an.[3]

❋

---

[1] XVIIIe et XIXe siècles: Saint Martin Carrefour des Antilles: étude socio-économique de la partie Française de Saint Martin. Gérard Lafleur. [2] Abraham Cannegieter, R. R. Richardson. [3] L'immuable et le changeant: étude la partie Française de Saint Martin, Yves Monnier. [4] Sualiga, Land of Salt: dossier de presse.

Salt production (1789-1961). Courtesy: Municipal Library salt exhibition, 1995.

"The laborers in the flats are allowed one hour in the morning for breakfast time, and another at noon for dinner, which time is made use of by them, or at least by most industrious, to reap salt for their own benefit, which they sell immediately to persons not having laborers of their own, obtain salt by purchase, the value of that article thus reaped is sold at the rate of nine Dutch cents per barrel, of three bushel measure. In quantity of salt reaped during the crop of 1789 may be conceived from the extent of the situation, on which the heap were placed, the whole extent of the pond side, as has already been mentioned, as allotments, nearly one English mile in length, had heaps of salt, each touching the other, not one heap containing less than one thousand barrels, the greater number, from four to five thousand, and one individual had a heap exceeding one hundred thousand barrels. It was estimated at the time, that over three millions of barrels were reaped.

"... (F)rom the account current book of the colonial treasurer of that land, by which it appears, ... from ... July 1789, to that of May 1790, a period of only eleven months, there was collected by duty on salt thirty thousand Guilders, and from the same source of information, that from the month of May 1789 to that of November 1792, only thirty one months, there was shipped from the port of Great Bay, seven hundred and five thousand barrels, from which the colonial government received two hundred and fifty six thousand, nine hundred and ninety eight Guilders.

"To such few persons, as were witnesses of the glorious crops of salt in 1789 and 1797 at the former period, when upwards of six thousand laborers were employed. ... It could not fail to be as source of grief to behold very often during the crop of 1837, not more than seventy or eighty laborers at work in reaping salt. ... In 1789, as much salt was reaped in one day, as the reduced and miserable beggared inhabitants in 1837 collected in three months.

"In the French part of the island, there are two ponds capable of making salt. One in the rear of the small fishing town of Grand Case ... but is not well situated. ... Being too much exposed to encroachments from the sea. There is also a small pond ... called Chevrus, well located for the making of salt which it does very frequently, that part of the island being much subjected to drought, the quantity of salt however, has never exceeded in a crop eight thousand barrels. ..."[10]

[9] *Written by St. Martin-born teacher and historical writer E. S. J. Kruythoff, circa 1938.*

[10] *"Sualouiga, The Land of Salt," Discover St. Martin/St. Maarten, 1995:98.*

St. Martin salt stock. Courtesy: Municipal Library salt exhibition, 1995.

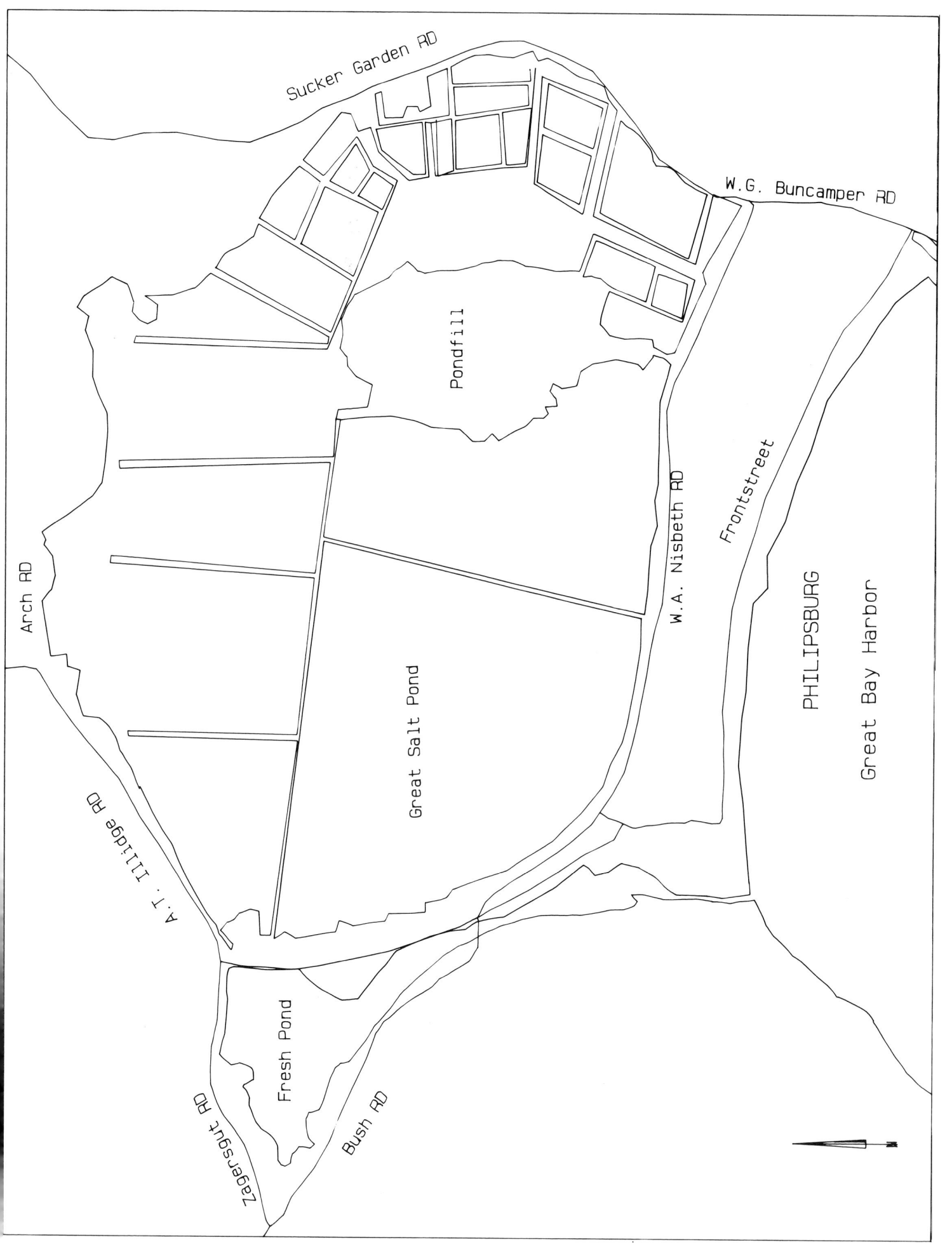

Source: Wing Surveys, 1996.

(The following was adapted with permission from STINAPA, Educational Letter Number 3, 1983.)

BIRDS OF THE POND

Many species of wading birds migrate south annually to escape the North American winter. For centuries, flocks of these birds have been reaching our friendly shores yearly. According to the Canadian Wildlife Service, St. Martin offers one of the most ideal winter residences for these birds. This is mainly due to our ponds, which, in a healthy state, teem with larval life, small fish, pond shrimps, and crabs, providing abundant food for the feathered guests.

"Pond birds," as St. Martiners tend to call all of the species collectively, create a glorious carnival of color, sound, and movement when they come to the pond sanctuaries of their seasonal island-home. The noisy stilts, the solemn crab-eaters, the royal great white herons, the industrious greater yellow legs, and the menacing man-o-war birds are some of the pond birds. These feathered creatures are important to the beauty and ecological health of our nation's precious environment. The waterfowls, as they are also called collectively, roost, feed, play, mate, and carry on all their "birdly" business almost oblivious to the surrounding human activities. The moment someone walks too close or stops his or her car nearby to admire the scenery, the flocks may come to attention and fly away at the slightest movement of the spectator.

In every pond, especially the Fresh Pond and Little Bay Pond, we will see or hear the green heron. While other birds will fly away silently if they spot unwanted visitors, the green heron disturbs the silence with alarming cries. Along with the stilt, the green heron can be considered the pond's watch-dog. All other birds come to attention when the green heron sounds the alarm and looks in the direction of the possible danger. The green heron is protected by law, breeds in St. Martin, and can be seen throughout the year. In some parts of the USA, the beautiful bird is called "lady-with-the-golden-slipper" because of the orange feet under its black legs.

Then there is the great white heron which is often confused with the cattle egret (white gaulin) often seen in pastures around grazing cattle. There are a number of other pond birds, such as the snowy egret, which we should become acquainted with. One high school's attempt in the 1980s to create a bird-watchers' park on the Fresh Pond's Zagersgut bank, was ravaged on September 5, 1995, by Hurricane Luis.

THE FRESHWATER LOBSTER

(Pondshrimp, Crayfish, Mudbag)

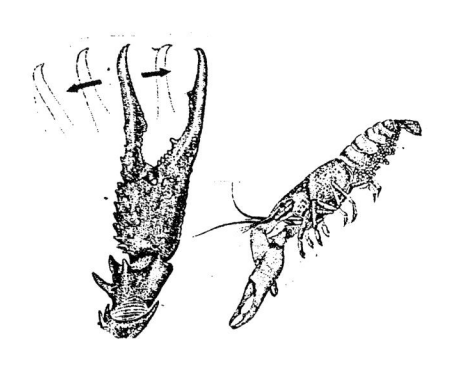

The crayfish is a freshwater cousin of the lobster. When walking along the bottom of freshwater ponds, it carries its two big pinchers upraised. If the crayfish senses danger, it flips its broad, powerful tail and zips off backward with a mighty thrust, leaving behind a swirling puff of stirred-up mud, thus the name mudbag.

Crayfish are amphibious and can travel long distances on land, especially during rain storms. Many crayfish appear after a heavy rainfall and flooding. In drier seasons, they burrow deep mud holes where they reside. After Hurricane Frederick passed in 1979, great numbers of crayfish appeared above ground in Dutch Quarter and French Quarter. They are quite appetizing when cooked. There are more than 300 species of this freshwater crustacean, including the giant Australian crayfish which grows to a foot and a half in length. Our St. Martin crayfish grows to ten inches in length (including its dark brown pinchers).

POND VEGETATION

Mangroves

When not disturbed by man, the shoreline pond vegetation shows a steady pattern of trees, shrubs, and weeds growing in one plant community. Most striking among the ponds' (and lagoon) plant community are the mangroves. Mangroves grow where land and water meet. Mangroves are flowering trees which can live in salt or brackish water and are, therefore, well-adapted to ponds, lagoons, swamps, and other areas flooded by water.

Among the types of trees referred to by the common name mangrove, the most recognized species are red mangrove, black mangrove, and white mangrove. A mangrove community may consist of red mangroves growing at the edge of a quiet shallow lagoon or pond; black mangroves on higher wet soil; and white mangroves, the least salt-tolerant, thriving on drier and higher inland soil.

The prop roots of the red mangrove *(Rhizophora mangle)*, extending far into the pond, and the saltpond tree or black mangrove *(Avicennia germinans [nitida])*, with its many air-roots popping out of the mud, can be seen on the shoreline of St. Martin's significant inland bodies of water. The buttonwood or button mangrove *(Conocarpus erecta)* is also one of St. Martin's wetland trees.

A proper mangrove growth can be found near Oyster Pond and in isolated areas along Simpson Bay Lagoon. The Fresh Pond and Friar's Bay Pond also have healthy mangrove growth. The most impressive mangrove is around Fish Pond in French Quarter. An extensive and rather deep fringe of mangrove trees borders the pondside of Baie de l'Embouchure. Extensive mangrove and other pond flora and fauna have been destroyed or are threatened in St. Martin by human activity. Mangrove stripped of their leaves by Hurricane Luis in September 1995, were rebounding in green splendor by April 1996.

The distinctive roots of mangroves, especially the red mangrove, trap sediment washed down from St. Martin's hillsides, particularly excavated land, during rain. By acting as a natural "strainer," mangroves prevent sediments and pollutants from leaving the ponds and lagoon, muddying the beach and coastal sea water and damaging reefs and seagrass beds. The black mangrove may also remove toxic chemicals from water before it runs into the sea. "The abundance of food and shelter makes the mangrove community one of the most biologically productive of tropical ecosystems. The trees also provide natural buffer zones that absorb the shock of hurricane waves and filter pollutants from fresh water runoff," wrote environmentalist Carroll B. Fleming. The Simpson Bay Lagoon and the pseudo-estuary in Oyster Pond provide ideal growing conditions for mangroves. Mangroves are like protective cribs in nature's lagoon and pond nurseries.

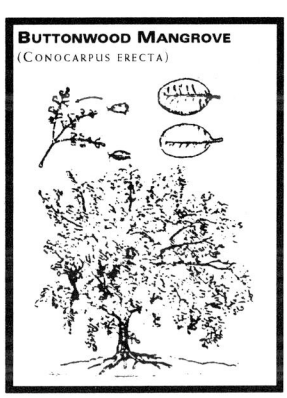

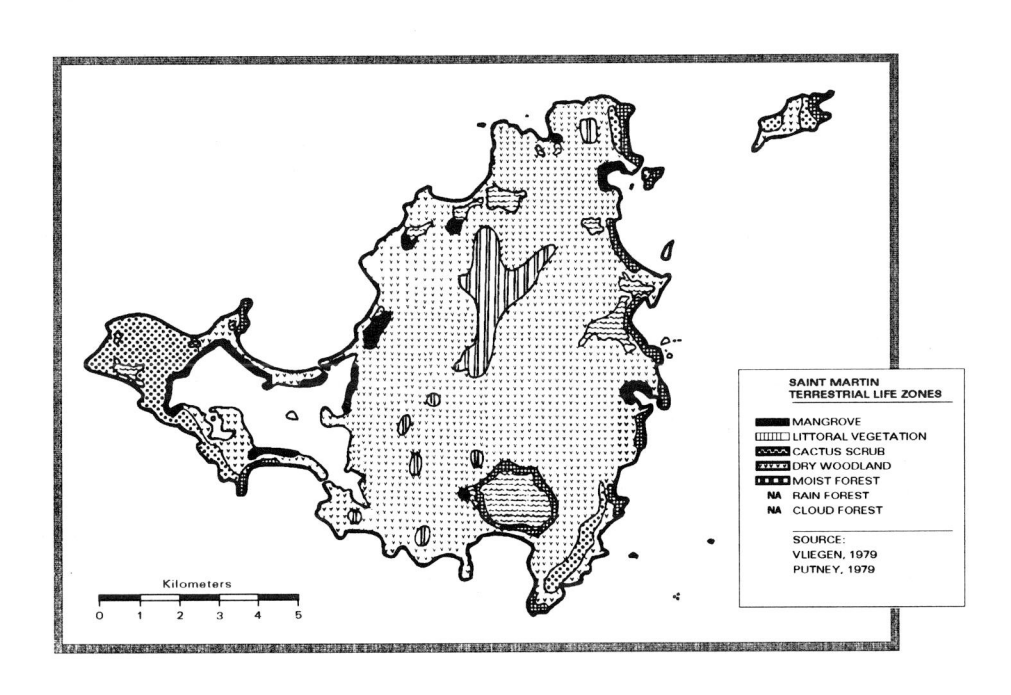

[Diagram with labels:]

MANGROVES help keep the water clean by filtering runoff and debris before it reaches the sea. Seagrasses and corals need clear water and good sunlight in order to thrive. They also serve as nursery areas for juvenile fishes and other marine marine animals.

ENVIRONMENTAL BOATING TIPS Avoid anchoring or operating your boat in or near seagrass beds. They are easily uprooted by anchors and boat props. Seagrasses are slow-growing, and do not recover quickly from such damage

SEAGRASSES and **MANGROVES** interact to provide important habitats for many species of fish and shellfish. Mangroves produce nutrients that support the growth of a number of other valuable marine ecosystems.

SEAGRASSES are very important. They help stabilize the seafloor in the same way grass does on your lawn. They help maintain water clarity, reduce beach erosion, and are the food source for marine animals like turtles and conch.

small turtle grass · manatee grass · turtle grass · shoal grass

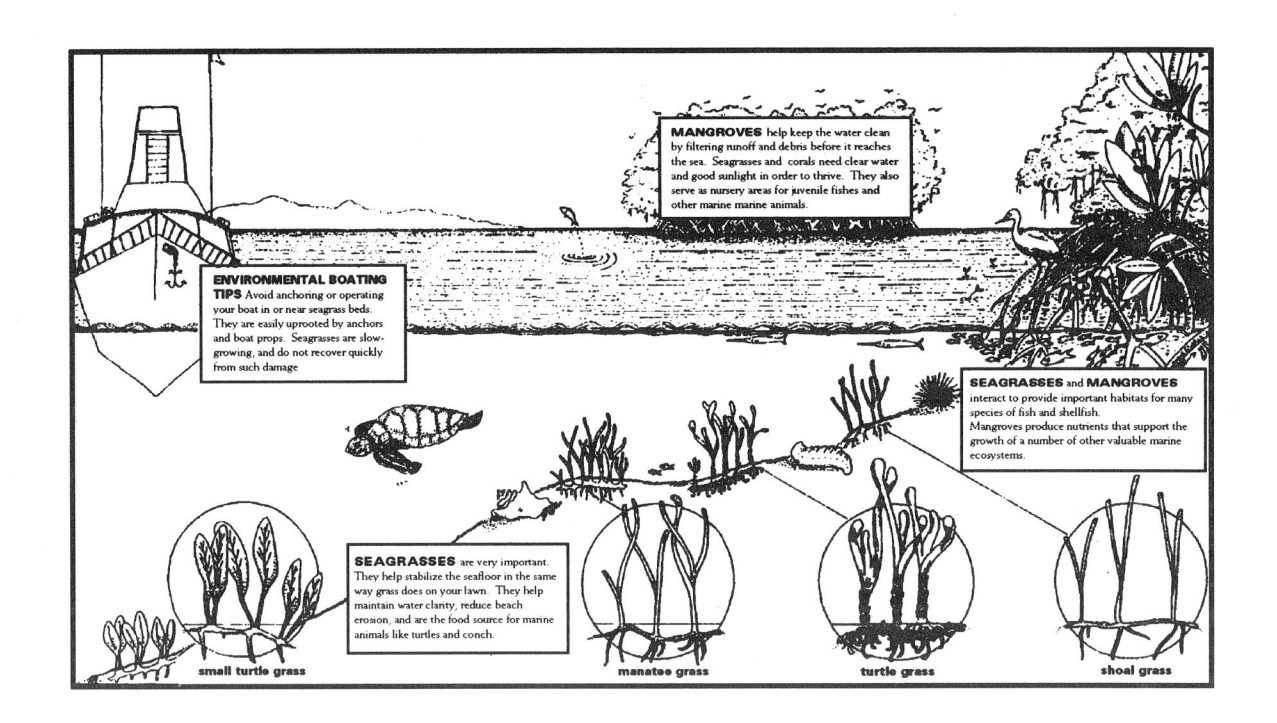

SIMPSON BAY LAGOON

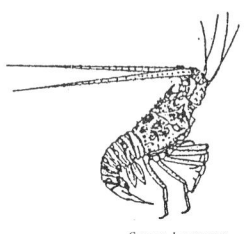

Spiny Lobster

Helmet Conch

St. Martin's most picturesque and impressive inland body of water is the Simpson Bay Lagoon. Along the banks of this grand lagoon are Simpson Bay, Mullet Bay, Lowlands, Sandy Ground, the city of Marigot, Low Town, St. Jean, and Cole Bay. (The lagoon is often nicknamed after the area it borders, i.e. "Cole Bay Lagoon," "Mullet Bay Lagoon," "Marigot Lagoon.") The vegetation-covered Great Key or Islet and Little Key are located in the lagoon. During the hurricane season, from June to November, Simpson Bay Lagoon is the primary safe haven, or hurricane hole, for small fishing boats and pleasure yachts.

Named after the old fishing village of Simpson Bay, the lagoon has for centuries served as a nursery for shrimp, lobster, conch, and juvenile reef and pelagic fish. Landfilling, dredging, refuse from yachts, piped-in sewage and leakage from the septic tanks of surrounding houses, hotels, restaurants, other businesses; are, at the time of this writing, polluting the lagoon and threatening mangroves and other life forms that depend on the lagoon.

Spanning 814.2 hectares in 1996, Simpson Bay Lagoon's

two outlets are to the Caribbean Sea and are located in the towns of Simpson Bay and Sandy Ground. A draw-bridge spans both narrow "canals" to the sea.

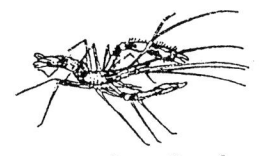

Along parts of Simpson Bay Lagoon's shoreline can be found extensive mangroves, especially the red mangrove (*Rhizophora mangle*). Mangroves, according to the Eastern Caribbean Center, sustain "... a complex food web beginning with micro-organisms and scavengers and culminating in such higher trophic members as snappers, barracuda, lobsters, and birds." Grunts, groupers, sea-trouts, silvers, and other commercially valuable fish are dependent on the mangroves in Simpson Bay Lagoon for breeding and much of their growing. Many species of birds are dependent on the lagoon for food and shelter.

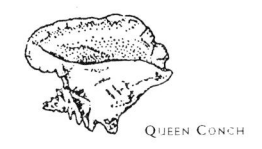

The Caribbean Conservation Association, which campaigns tirelessly to save the region's wetlands, reminds fishermen, governments, developers, and the general public that over sixty percent of Caribbean marine life, a main food source and major export commodity, is born in and grows up in the region's lagoons and other wetlands. Therefore, the concerns of Simpson Bay Lagoon Conservation Committee, Sint Maarten National Heritage Foundation, and other community-minded groups and individuals must be translated into greater public awareness, conservation activities, and government measures to protect Simpson Bay Lagoon. The lagoon must be protected from further pollution and other adverse affects of neighboring developments that "stress out" the life-giving body of water beyond its carrying capacity.

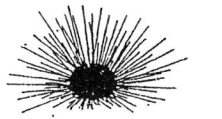

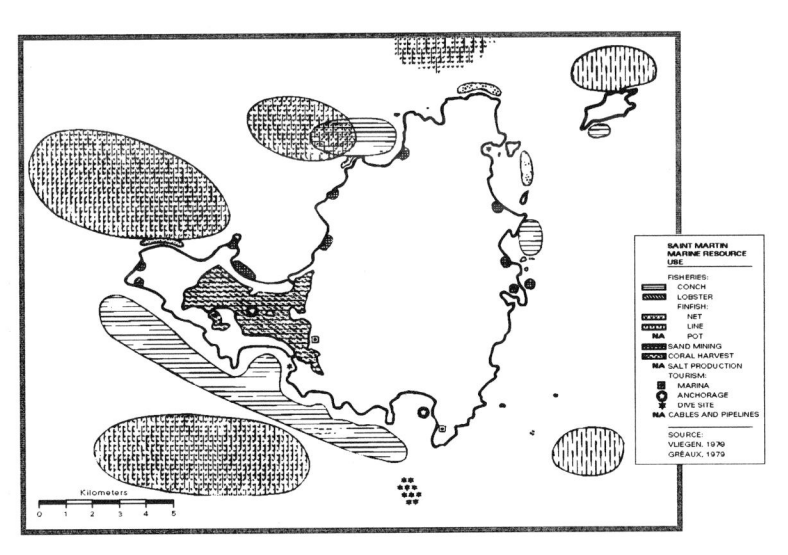

A healthy Simpson Bay Lagoon, in harmony with human development, guided by sound and pragmatic conservation policies and practices, will maintain the complex food chain on which air, land, and sea creatures rely. What will be assured is a scenic and healthy lagoon and lagoon environment and a continual supply of nutritious seafood for national consumption and export.

125

BEACHES OF ST. MARTIN

Beaches are usually attractive expanses of sand or pebbles along a seashore. The land extending from beaches often serves as prime property on which to build residences, hotels, and other recreational businesses. The thirty-seven-square-mile island of St. Martin and her islets have no fewer than thirty-two beautiful sand beaches!

Beaches are fundamental to St. Martin's environmental health, social/recreational infrastructure, and economic wealth. Our beaches are natural and national resources. It is in the interest of everyone to keep the beaches clean and conserved for the common good, including educational, creative social/recreational and tourism development. We must not allow our beaches to become private property, overdeveloped, polluted, or sold off to developers who try to prevent St. Martin's people, especially the Black population, from using certain beaches—as has been attempted in the not too distant past. Unobstructed access to all beaches and their free, safe, and fun use constitute a natural, civil, and human right.

Without proper conservation, the vegetation and wildlife of beaches can be destroyed by developments which over-tax the environment. Beaches are also under stress from waves, salt, spray-wind, and other natural phenomena. Sand may erode from the front of the beach and be carried offshore or along the shore. At other times, sand may be deposited on the beach. Certain beaches are more protected and stable than others. Nevertheless, they are all subject to change over a period of time.

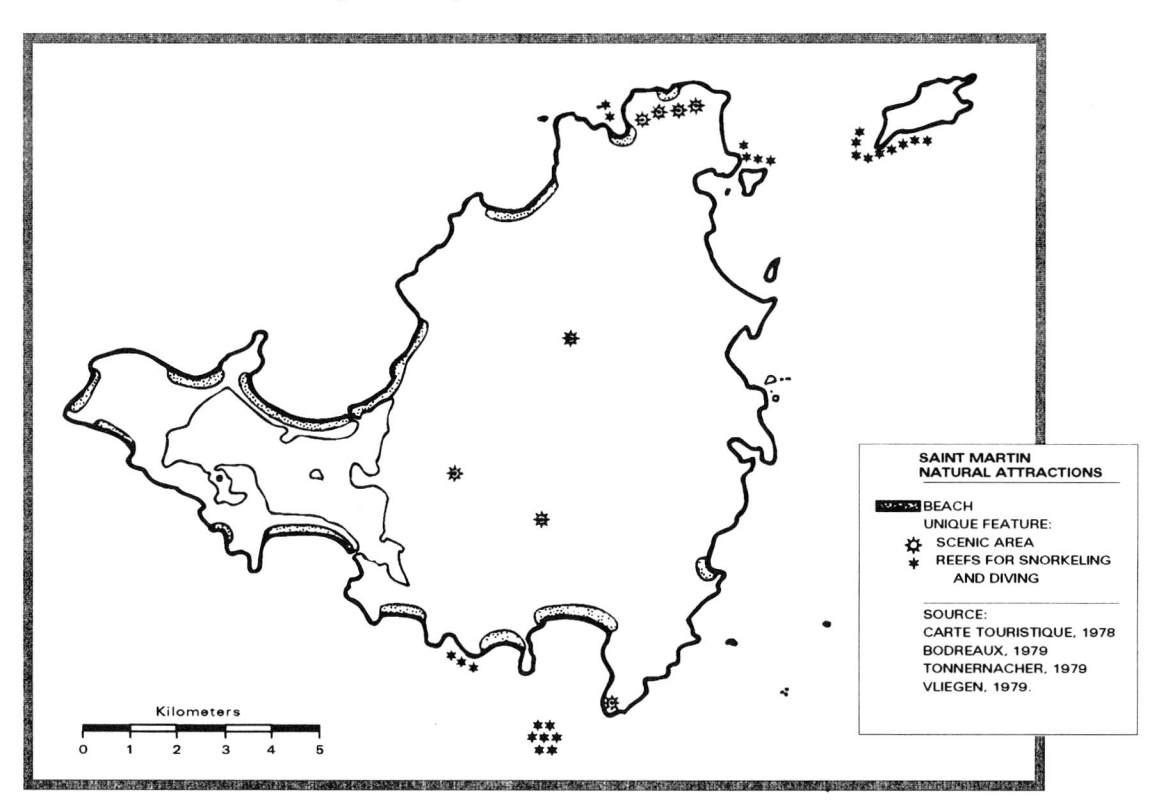

SAINT MARTIN
NATURAL ATTRACTIONS

BEACH
UNIQUE FEATURE:
☼ SCENIC AREA
✳ REEFS FOR SNORKELING AND DIVING

SOURCE:
CARTE TOURISTIQUE, 1978
BODREAUX, 1979
TONNERNACHER, 1979
VLIEGEN, 1979.

How beaches are made

Waves work endlessly to build and destroy beaches. Waves are "built" by the wind. Whenever waves come into a bay that has a sandy bottom, sand and other particles are transported to the shore. The last waves following the breakers and spillers dump the sand ashore. A good example of this beach-building process is at Guana Bay.

Sand beaches

St. Martin, Anguilla, and St. Barthelemy have an abundance of beaches, in part because these sister islands rise from a shallow part of the sea-bottom that is completely covered with sand. Sand grains on most of St. Martin's beaches are bits of quartz, the sand type most resistant to erosion. Quartz is like glass, decomposes slowly, and is the most common sand on earth.

Coral sand beaches

In tropical seas, coral reefs grow along the coast. Coral reefs are found on St. Martin's Atlantic coast, bordering the beaches and on the northwestern side, one thousand meters offshore. Most of St. Martin's beaches are white because they consist mainly of coral, limestone, and shell fragments. The fragments are crunched to small particles on the coral reefs and washed up on the beaches behind the reefs by wave action.

Reefs and coral sand beaches

Where there are coral reefs, there are beaches. When reefs are destroyed, beaches are destroyed. If a beach is destroyed and the reefs to which it is linked are intact, then the beach can be saved or restored.

Causes of reef destruction:

1. Dropping anchors from ships and boats on them.
2. Oil spillage.
3. Sewage-dumping.
4. Precipitation of soil from the land, caused by natural erosion, excavation, and deforestation.

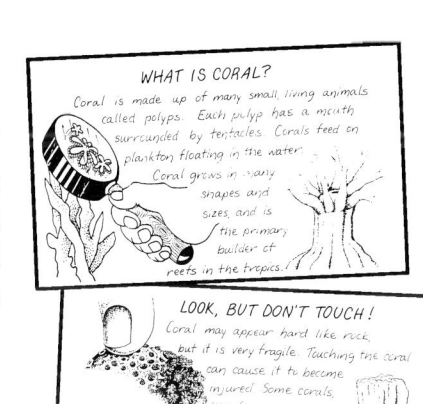

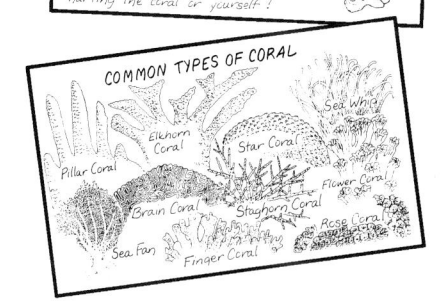

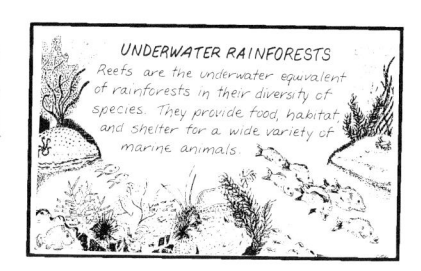

5. Brine from a water-producing plant.
6. Collection of live coral by divers.

The causes of reef destruction mentioned in this book will have adverse effects on beaches in the long run. It is essential for government planners, private developers, tourism officials, fishermen, environmentalists, educators, swimmers, beach picnickers, and vacationers to be sensitive to the complete beach environment. Some of St. Martin's reefs are showing signs of stress brought on especially by sewage-dumping.

Coral beaches

Coral beaches can be found behind the reefs, especially on the east side of the island where the sand is constantly washed away. The stones are gray because of exposure to sun, rain, and sea-spray for thousands of years. St. Martin's coral beaches are being destroyed because people have been removing the stones for construction. Removing sand from beaches weakens the shoreline, and as a result, a storm could do much damage.

Not all beaches are made of sand

Rock and pebble beaches will normally be found at the foot of cliffs. The waves "undermine" cliffs by breaking them away in vertical fashion. Cliffs affected by this process can be seen at Pointe Blanche and Red Bay (Baie Rouge).

Rock and pebble beaches

The stones on rock and pebble beaches are worn smooth as they grind against each other in the surf. One foot of rock may become sand in a few hundred years if kept in motion. Sand thus produced contains fragments of many rocks and minerals. The heavy surf deposits the rocks on the beach and washes the sand away. St. Martin's rock beaches are in hard-to-reach places such as Geneve Beach on the east coast. The rocks are made of hard Pointe Blanche formation.

Some beaches are not permanent

The phenomenon of temporary or seasonal beaches occurs in Cupecoy and Lowlands. During the first half of the year, the sand of Cupecoy beach is situated in front of the Cupecoy Beach condominium. In the second half of the year, changes in wind direction and hurricane swells "move" the sand to the other end of the beach. The wind direction is northeasterly from December to June and east-to-southeasterly from June to December. The Lowlands beaches facing southeast are affected mostly by southeasterly winds. The frequency of southeasterly winds changes from year to year, resulting in more or less radical beach shifts.

Impressive beach shifts occur in the area of Green Key. In the latter part of the year, a big sand spit juts southward, and in mid-year it is removed by the forces of nature and deposited alongside Green Key in a northeastern direction.

Why are our beaches so beautiful and clean?

One of the most important reasons why St. Martin has many clean and beautiful beaches is because there are no rivers depositing tons of mud and debris into the bays. However, in the last twenty-six years, according to STINAPA, "We are making our own mud rivers by ripping open our hills to build roads and houses and not taking care enough to prevent the soil from washing away into the sea. The ponds behind the beaches will take most of the mud but part of it is already reaching the bays." The once pristine, sparkling, white Great Bay Beach, at the time of this writing, includes significant and increasing deposits of mud. Piped in sewage and the yet unregulated dumping of refuse from yachts and other boats are also affecting the Great Bay reef and beach.

Taking sand from the beach

Sand is taken from the beaches regularly for building purposes. It is not true that "The sea deposits new sand right after you take some away." The sea will not deposit sand on the despoiled beach right away. For example, at Maho Beach, truckloads of sand have been taken away. As a result, the beach is receding and threatening the nearby road. Another bad practice is gathering sand behind the beach. This practice results in craters and a destroyed landscape.

BEACH PLANTS

Coconut tree

The coconut tree, that graceful palm lining tropical shores and widely planted for its fruit and landscaping, is a popular symbol of the tropics. The tree is one of the ten most useful trees to humankind.

The coconut tree is thought to have originated in South-East Asia. It is not known whether sea currents or early sailors transported the nuts of the tree to the Caribbean. There is no report of Christopher Columbus finding it. Most early Spanish writers in the New World did not mention it. Nevertheless, one hundred years after the European conquest, plunder, and colonization of the Caribbean began, the tree was growing at least in Puerto Rico, where coconut milk was used as "cosmetic for the ladies." On some islands, the coconut was not known until the seventeenth century.

COCONUT TREE

Sea grape

Plants that grow near the sea must be protected against salt. For this reason, most wild beach plants have thick, waxy leaves. The sea grape is one of the first line of trees growing on sandy shores. It is more salt-tolerant than most trees.

Healthy beaches will always have large stands of sea grape trees. The trees provide shade for beach guests, and protect the beach against excessive erosion from wave action and high winds.

Sea grape wood is preferred for making charcoal while jelly and wine are made from the fruit. Once upon a time, sea grape leaves were used as picnic "plates" by beach guests. St. Martin's children still make cone-shaped containers from the leaves to put the grapes in. Spanish colonists sometimes used the fresh, thick leaves as a substitute for paper, scratching messages with a pin, nail, or some other sharp object.

SEA GRAPE
(COCCOLOBA UVIFERA L.)

Manchineel

The manchineel, pronounced "mangeneedle" in St. Martin, is a salt-loving tree. The word manchineel is derived from the Spanish *manzanilla*, which means "little apple." The fruit, a small green apple, is poisonous. Even the leaves should be avoided. Never take shelter under a manchineel tree when it is raining. The raindrops that fall

RED GUM TREE
(BURSERA SIMARUBA L)

from the leaves will cause blisters on the human skin. There is a true story about Spanish soldiers who took off their shirts to chop down a forest of trees that covered the peninsula on which Fort Amsterdam now lays in ruins. The soldiers got sick after receiving blisters all over their skin. The trees that they chopped down in the boiling sun were mangeneedle trees.

The manchineel fruit, if eaten, may taste sweet at first, but soon the tissue of the mouth and throat will start to hurt severely. When the fruit reaches the stomach, it will produce a burning sensation. The next symptoms will be vomiting, extreme thirst, and a high fever. Eventually, a person who consumes a manchineel fruit will become unconscious and will die if not attended to by a doctor. A physician should be contacted immediately if anyone bites into or eats a manchineel fruit. Ancient Amerindians poisoned the tips of their arrows with the fruit's toxic, milky liquid.

LOCUST, STINKING TOE
(HYMENAEAE COURBARIL L)

HOGPLUM
SPONDIAS MOMBIN L)

KOSHA TREE

Sea vine

The creeping sea vine is a pioneer plant which establishes itself on the sandy shore. With its very long stems, it can cover considerable sandy surfaces. Its roots develop along the stems, anchoring the plant in the sand. A vast network of stems and leaves can grow like a protective cover over loose sand, preventing the wind from blowing away large amounts of dry sand. The plant bears flowers throughout the year. The stems contain white latex in abundance.

Milkweed
(Sprainleaf, Liberty Tree, Wild Cotton, French Cotton)

The peculiar, giant milkweed is more like a large herb than a tree. The large fruit is completely filled with silky hair which can be used to stuff pillows. The pink, waxy flowers remain for a long time on the plant, giving the milkweed a permanent decorative appearance. Traditional bush or herbal doctors used milkweed leaves to cure headaches. The leaves were wrapped in a cloth and the cloth tied around the patient's head as part of the treatment.

Other beach plants

St. Martin's coastal vegetation also includes the sea pea, sea lavender, silk cotton purslane, *Cakile lanceolate*, *Pedilanthus*, and yellow thistle *(Argemone mexicana)*.

BEACH BIRDS

The birds that can be found on mostly quiet beaches are migratory creatures. These birds travel annually from North America to the hemisphere's southern regions to avoid winter. St. Martin's salt-water bays, with their sandy beaches and vegetation, provide good habitats and feeding "grounds" for these birds.

Beach birds are generally difficult to spot. Their colored feathers blend harmoniously with the moist seaweed. This perfect blending of colors is called mimicry. In their search for food, beach birds scratch in heaps of sea-grass and seaweed swept onto the beaches by waves. If a person walks close by while beach birds were feeding, the vegetation would seem to come alive and the feeding flocks would fly away.

Among the beach birds found in St. Martin are tern, greater yellow leg, ruddy turnstone, black-bellied plover, and semi-palmated plover.

Beaches of St. Martin
Mullet Bay
Cupecoy (a string of beaches)
Long Bay (Baie Lounge)
Red Bay (Baie Rouge)
Marigot Bay
Friar's Bay
Happy Bay
Grand Case Beach
Grandes Cayes
Petite Plage (Grand Case)
Petites Cayes
Orient Bay (Nude Beach)
Marcel Cove Beach
Pinel Key Beach
Le Galeon
Dawn Beach
Great Bay Beach
Guana Bay
Maho Bay
Plum Bay
Nettle Bay
Galisbay
Cul-de-Sac Beach
Baie Blanche (Tintamarre Isle)
Baie de l'Embouchure (includes Coconut Grove Beach)
Lucas Bay
Cay Bay
Little Bay Beach
Belair Beach
Simpson Bay Beach

All of St. Martin's beaches are public.

ISLETS AND KEYS OF ST. MARTIN[11]

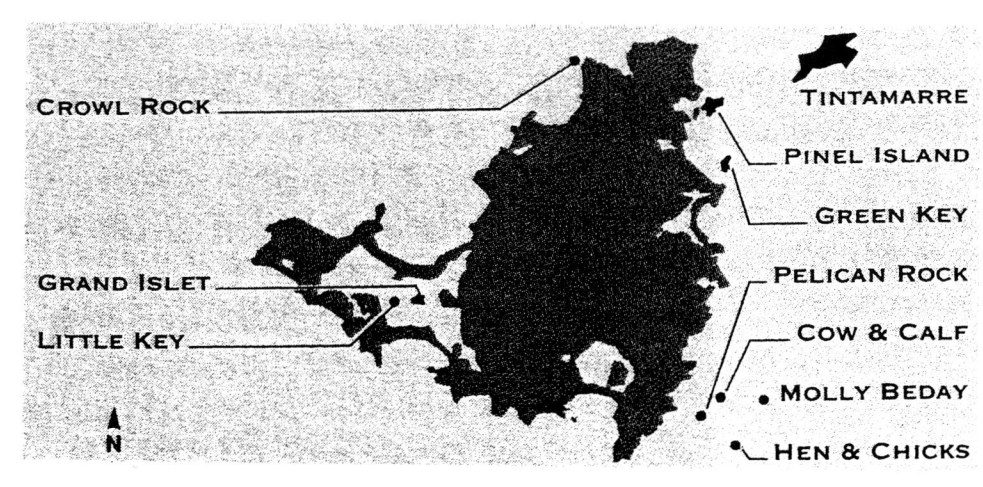

[11]Discover St. Martin/St. Maarten, 1991:76

THE BROWN PELICAN—NATIONAL BIRD OF ST. MARTIN

The brown pelican, along with the booby, tropicbird, and man-o-war, belongs to the order of pelicaniformes. There are six species of Old World pelicans and two New World species. St. Martin's national bird, the brown pelican, and the American white pelican are New World natives (*Pelecanus occidentalis* or pelican of the western hemisphere).

The pelican belongs to the order of pelicaniformes ("oar-footed") because skin grows between the bird's "toes" so that the feet may function as oars. This feature allows the pelican to paddle in water like a person uses oars to propel and steer a row-boat. The brown pelican spends most of its time at sea and in the lagoon and ponds of St. Martin and, therefore, needs the ability to swim.

Habitats, value, & symbols of the brown pelican

In North America, the brown pelican hugs the coasts, fishing almost exclusively in salt water. In the west, the bird's range extends south to Chile, and in the east, to the Guianas. Beyond the Guianas, this proud-looking and industrious bird would be unable to see his prey and fish for food because of the heavy concentration of silt pouring from Brazilian rivers into the Atlantic Ocean. Near the coasts of Peru and Ecuador, pelicans nest on the Chincha islands. There they are valued as the main producers of guano (bird manure), an important fertilizer.

In the United States of America, the pelican is the state bird of Louisiana—which is also called "Pelican State." In the Caribbean, the pelican adorns the crests or emblems of the University of The West Indies and the University of St. Martin. The noble bird is represented on Southern St. Martin's seal and flag and graces the emblem of the National Flag of St. Martin.

In St. Martin, our graceful-in-flight pelicans are seen in nearly every bay and in the lagoon and larger ponds. The main flocks reside on the eastern islets. Here we will find breeding colonies in March, April, and May. The Great Salt Pond, Fresh Pond, Little Bay Pond, and Grand Case Salt Pond are regularly visited by pelicans on the hunt.

History

The first Amerindians, Europeans, and Africans glanced at the brown pelican as we do today. Indeed, the pelican preceded the first human settlers to the island that is St. Martin.

Archaeological data show that the first known human settlers of the islands making up our Caribbean were peoples now generally referred to as Amerindians. Carbon dating of artifacts unearthed at Hope Estate (North) indicates that Amerindians settled St. Martin between 600 BCE and 560 BCE. Recent archaeological evidence indicates that the "Land of Salt" was visited over 3,500 years ago. The earliest settlers came to the region aboard seafaring vessels and may have originated in South America's Amazon Basin. They existed primarily by hunting, fishing, and gathering. Shortly after the beginning of the Christian Era (AD), a more sophisticated group entered the Caribbean from South America. A few hundred years before Christopher Columbus and his crew "stumbled" into the archipelago aboard the Niña, Pinta, and Santa Maria, another group, which is known as Island Caribs, arrived.

The reputedly war-like Caribs, who overpowered earlier settlers, including some Arawakan nations and tribes, resisted European encroachment for at least two hundred years. However, the independence-loving Carib defenders (of their "newly" acquired or captured island-homes) could not match the equally war-like European conquistadors, traders, adventurers, missionaries, governments, and colonialists in fire-power and barbarity. The Caribs at times formed alliances with Maroon Africans, also called runaway slaves, against European colonialists. In St. Vincent, led by such noted *caciques* or chiefs as Chatoyer, the two peoples managed at one time to rid the island of their European oppressors. The Garifuna or Black Caribs in Central America are descendants of the union forged between both proud peoples.

The Island Caribs are vilified in the European's history of the Caribbean probably because of the comparative boldness of their resistance to European domination. There are the dogged tales of Carib cannibalism enshrined in European literature on the region. These stories were supposedly first told to Europeans by Arawaks who were long fed up with Carib aggression. Today, the false tale of Carib cannibalism survives with much vehemence. It is repeated in Caribbean school books and classrooms as a result of ignorance and lazy scholarship. It is reinforced in tourist brochures probably to add a measure of exoticism but amounts to nothing more than racism.

W. Arens's masterful book, *The Man-Eating Myth*, dispels the notion and nonsense of cannibalism as a diet of any people. If there is the slightest evidence that warrior "societies" of any ancient nation or tribe engaged in the ritual eating of a slain enemy's body parts, then Germanic tribes will be found no more innocent than, say, Pacific islanders. (The latter peoples have also been stigmatized as cannibals and "head hunters" by European sailors, writers, conquerors, and Christian missionaries who were themselves "devouring" the land and culture of the so-called "savage natives.") Island Caribs, from whom the region derives its name, survive in small numbers in Trinidad and St. Vincent. Caribs live on a reservation in Dominica. Archaeologists and anthropologists now question the direct relation between Island Caribs and the Caribs or Kalinago peoples of Venezuelan and Guyana.

In the ancient Caribbean, Ciboney, Arawak, Taino, Island Carib, and other Amerindian peoples appear to have depended far more on the sea than on the land. Their staple consisted mainly of conch, crab, and fish. An important bird to especially the Arawaks was the pelican. From the beginning of Amerindian settlement, the oar-footed one's image was being carved in stone. Animals and birds were often fashioned on every-day pottery and jewelry. The pelican's image may have represented magic to influence the hunting or fishing in the wearer's favor, especially since the pelican would have been seen as a wonderful fisherbird.

The Arawaks, like all ancient peoples, believed in the existence of benevolent and evil spirits which inhabited natural objects. They believed that by controlling spirits of nature, they would gain supernatural powers. Thus they fashioned icons of wood, stone, shell, cotton, and pottery in which these spirits could reside. Archaeologists show that many birds were hunted for meat or feathers, but there is no evidence that the pelican was ever preyed upon by Amerindian peoples. Artifacts bearing Amerindian icons have been found in St. Martin. They are on permanent exhibition at On the Trail of the Arawaks museum in Marigot. Amerindian finds are part of St. Martin's national patrimony and can be considered prized examples of early Caribbean art.

Features of the brown pelican

Seldom is a sound uttered from the pelican's ponderous bill. This enormous beak consists of the upper mandible, which is flat, and the lower mandible, which has a stretched pouch. This pouch serves as a scoop, not as a storehouse. After a plunge in the ponds, lagoon, or sea by this bird, the water is drained between mandibles. The bird points his bill skyward and the fish caught slides down his gullet.

The color variations of "Old Browny" tell about his age. The white-capped birds are adults. Females and males look alike. The brown-capped birds are juveniles. Pelicans nest in colonies on quiet, rocky islands.

Pelicans build their nests on bare ground, in the manchineel (mangeneedle) tree flattened by wind or in sea grape trees. The bottom of pelican nests is often cemented with the bird's excrement, also called guano. Both parents incubate the 1x4-inch chalk-white eggs for about thirty days after they are laid by the mother bird. This prehistoric-looking bird is born "naked" and blind. After a few days, the chicks will grow white down. Two weeks later, pelican chicks leave the nests and form noisy juvenile groups. The chicks are fed fish by their parents until they are able to fly.

Hunting or fishing is a busy activity for older pelicans. To see these birds plunging from great heights to the sea, ponds, or lagoon is a glorious spectacle. The clash with the water surface is so great that fish in the immediate area will become temporarily dazed. While diving from the sky into the water to catch fish, the brown pelican uses air-sacs to break its landing. The air-sacs, located in the bird's breast, absorb tremendous shock upon impact with the water.

Protecting the brown pelican

In 1903, Pelican Island in Florida's Indian River was set aside "... as a reserve and breeding ground for native birds ...," which included mainly the brown pelican. Commercial fishermen, mindful of the pelican's fondness for fish, frequently raided the bird colony, killing the birds and scattering their nests. Investigators proved, however, that pelicans were not competing with fishermen for food but ate mostly trash fish. Thus the birds were spared.

St. Martin's pelicans were, until very recently, shot regularly more for sport than food. This happens less frequently now. However, there are still fishermen who catch the birds and cut open their stomach to take out bait for their lobster-pots. Killing the brown pelican is a crime under the law (Netherlands Antilles). It is important to protect the breeding colonies of the brown pelican. These birds may indicate the healthiness of the sea and marine life. Fishermen should therefore learn to coexist with nature for the benefit of all. Take pride in St. Martin's natural and national symbols. Respect and protect the Brown Pelican.

MORE BIRDS OF ST. MARTIN

St. Martin is populated and visited every year by a number of other wild bird species. Author S. J. Kruythoff wrote of sixty-five species known to St. Martin, Saba, and St. Eustatius. By the early 1900s, a number of St. Martin's native birds such as the wild fowl, wood-pigeon, crested plover, wood-dove, and blue pigeon, were exterminated. Many "birds of passage" had ceased their annual visits. Game hunting, "desiccation of streams, pools and ponds. ... Bush rats—which nest in trees—the mongoose, and the lack of laws to protect game birds are the sole cause of this pitiable extinction." Bellow are listed some of the wild birds that can still be found in St. Martin—cited by their insular or species names.

BLACKBIRD	(Species: Carib Grackle [*Quiscalus lugubris*]; other names in the Caribbean: Bequia; Merle)
CATTLE EGRET	(*Bubulcus ibis*; other names in the Caribbean: Cattle Gualin; Garza Africana)
CHICKEN HAWK	(Species: Red-tailed Hawk [*Buteo jamaicensis*]; other names in the Caribbean: Malfini; Guaraguao)
COLLARED PLOVER	(*Charadrius collaris*)
GROUND DOVE	(Species: Common Ground Dove [*Columbina passerina*])
GUINEA-FOWL	(Species: Common Guinea-Fowl [*Numida meleagris*]; other names in the Caribbean: Guinea Bird; Gallina de Guinea)
HUMMINGBIRD	(Species not known to editor; called "Founfoun" in Northern St. Martin)
KILLY-KILLY	(Species: American Kestrel [*Falco sparverius*]; other names in the Caribbean: Killy Hawk; Gri-gri; Kinikini)
LESSER BLACK-BACKED GULL	(*Larus fucus*)
MANGROVE CUCKOO	(*Coccyzus minor*; in his research, James Bond says that this bird is a vagrant to St. Martin)
MOUNTAIN DOVE	(Species: Zenaida Dove [*Zenaida aurita*])
POND BIRD	(Species: Willet [*Catoptrophorus semipalmatus*]; this may be the 'Laughing Bird' cited by Kruythoff; other names in the Caribbean: Long-legs; Laughing Jackass; Chorlo)
SPARROW	(Species not known to editor; Insular name Chee-chee)
SPOTTED CRAKE	(*Porzana porzana*; according to Bond, this initially migratory bird to the Caribbean may no longer be considered vagrant to some islands but "native" instead)
THRUSH	(*Magarops fuscatus*)
TROPICBIRD	(*Phaethontidae*)
YELLOW-BREAST	(Species: Bananaquit [*Coereba flaveola*]; other names in the Caribbean: Paw-paw Bird; Sugar Bird; Siguita)

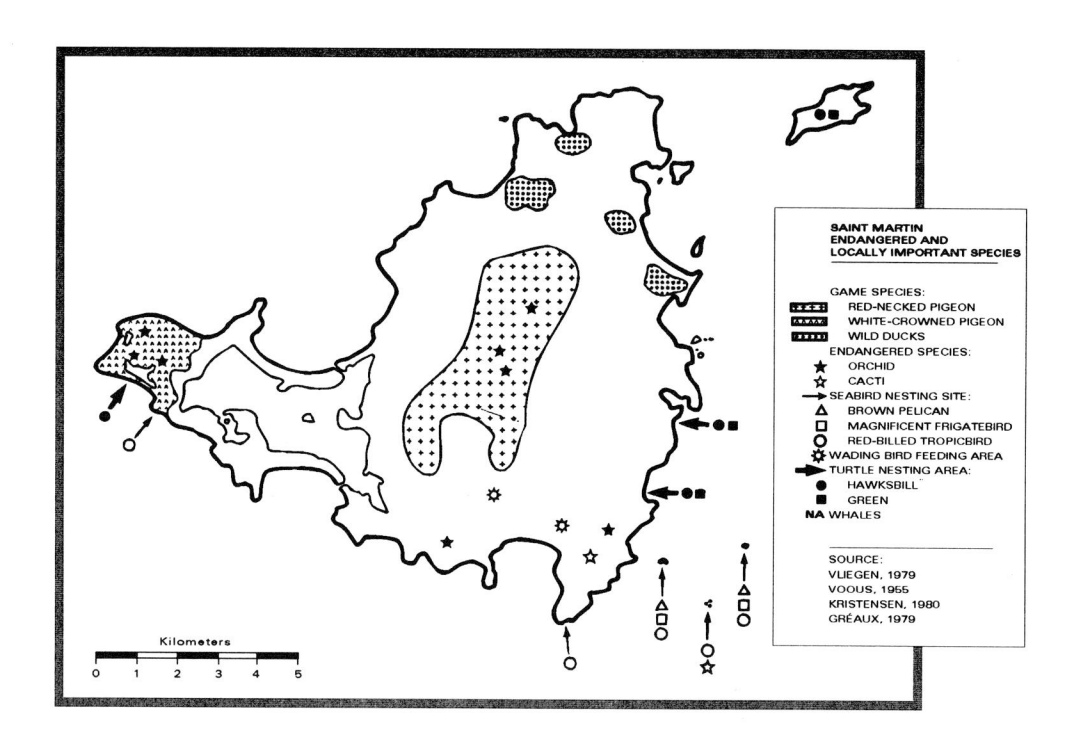

TREES AS CULTURAL MONUMENTS

The tamarind tree and other plant life of St. Martin have been endowed with cultural, spiritual, historical, environmental, ornamental, medicinal, and even cadastral significance. Our trees, plants, and flowers are thus natural and national resources and symbols.

To writer Camille Baly, "There are trees ... which are monuments" within the matrix of Traditional St. Martin and have survived as definitive cultural elements. Among the survivors is "The baobab ... known as a tree found in West Africa and of which there are possibly only three still standing in Simartn.[12] ... The baobab was revered by the slaves. It is said that the souls of good people, especially the griots (African story-tellers), reside in the trunk of this rare tree. ...

"Other trees linked with the people's concern are the silk cotton, the sandbox, and the flamboyant. ... The impressive silk cotton tree presents an ominous picture with its labyrinth root-formation, and as expected, has been associated with high powers. It is thought to be the abode of jumbies. ... The flamboyant tree, also called 'July Tree,' has special significance to the Simartner since it is associated" with enforcement of the abolition of slavery in "July for both sections of the island ... when the flamboyant or poinciana *(was)* in full bloom. The sandbox was the tree under which the slaves found a shade to rest, and, therefore," it was never to be cut down. The sandbox tree leaf is illustrated on the National Flag of St. Martin.

Two other "monument" trees of St. Martin are the red gum tree and the guavaberry tree. The red gum tree (*Bursera simaruba*), like the tamarind tree "... is ... a marker for boundary points of property." Traditional healers or "Bush Doctors," and many grandmothers, prepared a tea from red gum tree leaves for colds, coughs, and venereal diseases. A 1982 STINAPA report on trees stated that the tree provides a cure for gastric and duodenal ulcers. Ancient Amerindians made their canoes waterproof with the red gum tree's resin and extracted a glue and fuel for torches. It is thought that the tree also acts as an insect repellent.

[12] *A written form of the native pronunciation of St. Martin. The pronunciation is also written S'maatin.*

Guavaberry tree

The guavaberry tree, or rather its fruit, is inextricably linked to St. Martin's festive culture. The ever-green guavaberry tree may have gotten its name from the peeling or flaking off in plates of its bark, a characteristic of the guava tree. The guavaberry tree, also known as "mirto," is found at low altitudes in the Caribbean and South America—covering a range from Cuba to eastern Brazil where it grows wild to about fifty-five feet high.

The guavaberry fruit matures between December and April. The aromatic fruit, which may be red or yellow, is round and measures some 3/8 inch in diameter. It is from this little fruit that St. Martin's most famous and "mature" drink is made.

St. Martiners exported demijohns of guavaberry liqueur throughout the first half of the 1900s. Since the 1980s, entrepreneur Stephen Thompson has been adding to that history for his dedication to the national drink as a quality domestic and export product. According to Thompson, "The legendary island folk liqueur of St. Martin ... has been made in private homes for hundreds of years." To St. Martiners, "Guavaberry conjures up treasured memories of the olden days. There are folk songs and stories celebrating Guavaberry. This simple, fresh, wild fruit liqueur actually became an essential feature of the folklore of the island. Guavaberry is made from rum and the ... berries. The fruit is found high in the warm hills in the centre of the island. The mature liqueur has a woody, fruity bitter-sweet flavour all of its own."

In 1992, Tanny & The Boys stringband immortalized a version of the traditional "guavaberry song" with *Fête – The First Recording of Traditional St. Martin Festive Music*.

Tamarind tree

The tamarind tree originated in Africa and was brought to the Caribbean in the early seventeenth century.

The tree was planted for its fruit, landscaping, and the generous shade it provided from the sun. The wood was used mainly for fuel. It is believed to generate intense heat. In some countries, the wood is used to make furniture and other articles but it is considered very difficult to work with. Formerly, crushed charcoal from tamarind wood was used to make gunpowder.

Tamarind is pronounced "tamon" in St. Martin, where under the grand tree, popular jumbie stories were told at night well into the 1960s. The legendary story-teller, Ton'ton Butty, spun his tales under a "tamon" tree in Rambaud. Some folk-tales tell of jumbie families doing the "Jumbie Dance" on full moon nights under certain "tamon" trees of St. Martin.

Candy, preserves, and "tamon" juice are prepared from the tart pulp of the tamarind fruit. The pulp, which may be eaten fresh, is contained in a pod. The pulp has medicinal value and was used in olden times as a laxative or "blood cooler." Large quantities of St. Martin's "tamon" fruit, according to writer Camille Baly, were once exported to the United States of America for use in the preparation of medicine. Besides making the tree look beautiful when in bloom, the tamarind's flowers attract bees and are an important source of honey. In India, tamarind trees are planted on forest fire-breaks because the ground underneath the tamarind is usually bare. This may have been one of the reasons why "the trees were also markers for plantations" in St. Martin. Able to survive long spells of drought, the tree is strongly recommended for reforestation in dry Caribbean regions. Germination of the seeds occurs within ten days. Handling the seed does not require special attention. When planted in cultivated soil, the tamarind seeds and young plants should be protected against goats, sheep, and cattle. In the wild, seedlings do not survive because of these animals.

St. Martin's tamarind population is slowly aging, warned STINAPA in 1982. Great care should be taken not to chop down the tamarind tree, and additional trees should be planted. The tamarind leaf and fruit are depicted on the emblem of the National Flag of St. Martin.

Etching: "The Baobab," by Roland Richardson.

PLANT A TREE

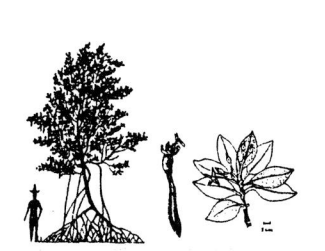

The Caribbean Conservation Association encourages individuals, groups, schools, and governments to "plant a tree" to halt and reverse the global crisis of deforestation. Plants provide temporary shelter, habitat, medicine, and food for humans and St. Martin's cattle, goats, sheep, mongoose, guinea-fowl, birds, lizards, insects, and other animals. Trees control flooding and protect precious topsoil from running off the hillside and arable land, onto the beaches and into the ponds, lagoon, and eventually, into the sea, causing harm and destruction to reefs and fish.

According to the United States Environmental Protection Agency: "Trees and other plants make their own food from carbon dioxide in the atmosphere, water, sunlight, and small amounts of soil elements. In the process, they release oxygen for us to breathe. Trees help settle out, trap, and hold particulate pollutants (dust, ash, pollen, and smoke) that can damage the human lungs. Particulates are trapped and filtered by leaves, stems and twigs, and are washed to the ground by rainfall." Trees contribute to the "environmental, economic, and social well-being" of our country.

St. Martin's flora, in addition to those specifically mentioned in this book, include marrow or Croton flavescens—which Dr. Hendrik van Rijgersma catalogued during the 1800s as the dominant species in the plains and lower hills; Acacia, Solanum, and Capparis species; sage (*Lantana camara*), jumbie beans, eyebright (*Heliotropium indicum*); Lowlands vegetation such as the many cacti; hill vegetation such as the locust tree (*Hymenaea*), dogwood (*Piscidia*), black berry, also called Caribbean Cherry (*Eugenia*), *Zanthoxylum*, *Hura crepitans*, hibiscus, bromelia, and orchid species. The vitamin-rich mango, guava, kinnip (genip), pommeserette, cherry-nut (cashew), cherry (*Malpighia punicifolia*), lime, papaya, sugar apple, mammy apple, and other fruits are all grown on trees which still form part of our natural environment and need to be cultivated and conserved.

In addition to their known and unknown medicinal value, trees, plants, flowers, and shrubs beautify the landscape and enhance property value, take in carbon dioxide in the process of growing, help keep the island's air clean, reduce soil erosion, the greenhouse effect and global warming.

So plant a tree, especially a fruit-bearing tree for human consumption. Cultivate flower-bearing plants in the front yard of your house, church, around public buildings, hotels, apartment buildings, private businesses, and along public roads. Plant a provisions/vegeta-

MANGROVE TREE
RHIZOPHORA MANGLE L.)

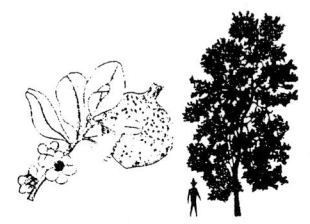

MAMMY APPLE
(MAMEA AMERICANA L.)

WHITE CEDAR
(TABEBUIA PALLIDA, MIERS)

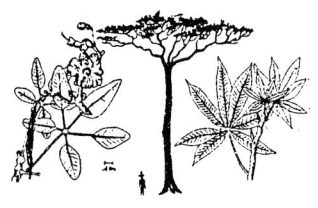

SILK COTTON TREE
(CEIBA PENTANDRA L.)

bles and fruit garden in your backyard and school yard. There is no reason why Great Bay and Marigot should not be "landscaped" into green cities.

Planting or replanting to develop a healthy flora community will even help wildlife that are nearly extinct or absent from the island to make a come-back. Take for example, butterflies. Among the most fragile of species, butterflies exist primarily to cross-polinate flowers. Some flowers and plants depend almost entirely on the tiny creatures. They are part of the food chain for other animals. A plant environment under stress from human activities, such as the spraying of certain insecticides, will wipe out butterflies and destroy or reduce the number of animals and plants dependent on them. In addition to being a feast for human eyes, butterflies may also tell us about the quality of the air we breathe.

In fact, some of the folks at The Butterfly Farm in Orleans think that St. Martin may have lost the zebra (*Charitonius heliconid*) and flame (*Dryas julia*) butterflies in the 1950s and 1960s when the island was heavily sprayed with D.D.T. Butterflies cannot fly over the sea and the farm has imported a few from Saba and St. Eustatius for its exhibit, and with the hope of reintroducing the species. Interestingly, after years of absence in abundance, in early 1996, following weeks of rain, butterflies were seen in great numbers throughout the island.

It is also important to consider replanting some of the species of trees that were of great economic import in the formation of the nation. Caribbean or West Indian Mahogany (*Swietenia mahogani*) and Tree of Life (*Lignum vitae*) were used extensively for construction and boat building. St. Martin's White Cedar (*Tababuia pallida*), from which many homes were built, still colors our hills with pink morning glory-like flowers, even during dry spells. Although changes in public preferences for trees have shifted to imported varieties, nurserymen like those at Greenfingers try to propagate and sell St. Martin varieties.

GUAVABERRY LEAVES AND FRUIT

Emilio's, on L. B. Scott Road. Formerly a plantation house of John Philips and the van Romondts. Pen & ink by F. de Kock. Courtesy: Sint Maarten Museum.

SUGAR PLANTATIONS OF MARIGOT

In 1988, the French Ministry of Culture requested a survey of the sugar plantations of France's remaining colonies in the Caribbean. The Research Unit in Industrial Archeology of the University of the Antilles-Guyana, charged with conducting the survey, commissioned professors Demise and Henrik Paresis to compile the data on the now defunct plantations of Northern St. Martin. The Cultural and Historical Foundation of St. Martin collaborated with the researchers. An extract from the extensive investigation appeared in the 1992 issue of Discover St. Martin/St. Maarten and was adapted with permission and developed by the editor of this book to give a brief micro-view of the Sugar Plantation Era in St. Martin. The complete survey dossier was deposited at the Municipal Library in Marigot.

There is to date no comprehensive record of the sugar plantations in the North of St. Martin before 1772. A 1797 census gave a description of "private" plantations, or *habitations* as they were called but cited nothing about sequestered plantations. However, because of the near complete record of notary deeds from 1775 onward, there can be a thorough survey or inventory, and inferences made, about the rise and fall of the Sugar Plantation Era in St. Martin.

A historical overview

The first plantations in St. Martin, particularly in the North, started growing sugarcane and producing sugar, molasses, and rum around 1765, just after the Seven Years' War (1756-1763) between France and England. By 1767, French sugar exports exceeded British exports in the Caribbean. In *U.S. Policy in the Caribbean*, John Bartlow Martin is succinct: "During the English-French rivalry of the eighteenth and early nineteenth centuries, the Caribbean, and its sugar, was the critical prize. ... Sugar had always been the central economic force in the Caribbean. The price of sugar in the world market meant economic life or death; and sugar was linked to race, slavery, and colonialism." To noted scholar George Lamming, "It is almost impossible to do justice to the unique brutality of thought and feeling which became the European consciousness in its insatiable hunger for gold which by the eighteenth century had transformed sugar into the value of steel and oil in our time."

Most of the plantations in the North of St. Martin were on land granted by the French governor, Augustin Descoudrelles, to

Spring sugar plantation ruins, by Cozbi Cabrera.

Europeans who wished to settle in St. Martin, no matter their religion or country of origin. This policy proved fruitful, and by 1794, thirty-one plantations were counted in the North of the island, with an average area of about one hundred squares each. Forty squares of each grew sugarcane. (A square is approximately one hectare.) The former resources of the island—cotton, tobacco, cattle, and food crops—had lost ground. Salt was also a major export product but primarily so in the South of the island. During this period, English became the common language and Protestants made up the largest religious group.

African peoples, especially from West Africa, were pressed into brutal slavery and made up St. Martin's numerical majority. Africans were in St. Martin from the late 1620s. The European minority constituted the bulk of the rich, armed, and exploitative class which owned the plantations and salt-pans. Among the Africans known to have been kidnapped and brought in chains to St. Martin were the noble Ashanti and peoples from the Guinea area. Peoples from many other African tribes, states, and kingdoms were sold into slavery in St. Martin and throughout the hemisphere.

European colonialists tortured, and sometimes killed Africans in the Caribbean if they spoke the African languages, used their original names, practiced their religions, or showed any love for or physical expression of their culture publically. (Brazil, Suriname, Cuba, Jamaica, Haiti, Trinidad, and Grenada [its island of Carriacou], are among the countries where remnants or important African traditions "survive," making it comparatively easy to trace aspects of the "cultural" ancestry of significant numbers of the citizenry to specific African tribes, nations, or past kingdoms.) The 1863 census registry in Great Bay refers to "Congo" as a first name. That name might have been a proud attempt by an ancestor to keep some aspect of the original home and identity alive. In one surviving legend, a St. Martin family claims to be the progeny of a kidnapped African princess.

The French Revolution in 1789, and the Haitian Revolution which began in 1791, with a mass slave revolt in Hispaniola's wealthy North Province, started a process which, by 1795, had caused enough disruptions in the slavery-based economy to signal that its death was not far off.[13] In 1795, still in the throes of a revolution which "popularized the rights of bourgeois man" but "proved enigmatic in the colonies," the French captured the island of St. Martin. Plantations owned by Englishmen and French nobles were sequestered. A number of royalists fled the island. Many nobles and other planters who did not support the French Revolution were jailed. The sugar plantations, then called *Habitations de la Republique*, went on working. Blacks, especially in the North, became free land-tillers under a supervisor called a *sequestre*. The supervisors were chosen more for their republican leanings than for their agricultural skills. (A few Blacks were enlisted in the French Army.)

In 1801, the majority of St. Martin's Blacks, without arms, disenfranchised, socially unorganized, without economic power and access to formal education, and thus unable to defend their own freedom, were forced back into slavery when the English invaded and controlled the island until 1802.

From 1795, to 1802 when Napoleon Bonaparte re-established slavery, the growth of the island's sugar industry was slowed. A few merchants and planters left the island and never came back. In 1808, the English returned to occupy St. Martin for a short while. The island-wide famine of 1809 left two hundred Blacks and a few poor whites dead. The famine, brought on in part by American-English-French trade disputes which led to the American Embargo Act of 1807, and the Non-intercourse Act of 1809, made basic foods scarce and reduced the money made on sugar exports.

The British invaded again in 1810, and were not routed until 1816. The Blacks were kept slaving away under the whip, salt-pans, plantations, and sugar mills kept producing, the white planters (often absentee) and merchants kept profiting. The European governments, royal families, and mercantile class of the day continued to be enriched. The island's population in 1816 was 9000 people (7000 enslaved Blacks, 1000 "coloreds"—which included free Blacks and mulattoes—and 1000 whites). Thirty plantations belonging to twenty-eight owners were recorded in the North, compared to twenty-eight plantations owned by twenty-five landlords in the South. In 1819, it is estimated that there were thirty-four sugar plantations in the North of the island. Cotton was still losing ground.

The 1819 hurricane and earthquake brought a dramatic change. Many smaller plantations were completely ruined. The wealthier planters bought these properties at a low price. The already oppressive conditions of Blacks worsened. *Marronage* and *petite marronage* increased. Some white families got richer; some landowners became impoverished and left the island; recent European immigrants bought properties to become sugar planters

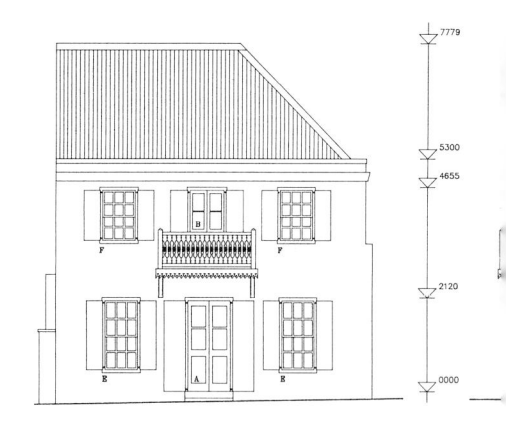

Restored part of Com. W. Rink's house, built between 1720-80, Frontstreet 29. Source: PLAN'D2, 1993.

and slave owners. A few landlords owned as many as three hundred squares of cane fields (the French-controlled North of St. Martin measured 3,500 squares, and half of that was available for sugarcane production). The post-1819 consolidation of properties did away with many sugar mills, and two mills destroyed by the hurricane were not rebuilt. Sugar production in the Dutch-controlled South continued to decline and never after topped the 1,400,000 pounds recorded for the very prosperous 1816-1818 period.

Sugar plantations in the Marigot quarter

No records have yet been found of plantations in Marigot prior to 1766. However, two plantations were recorded by 1769, and seven in 1772. The 1772 census, conducted by governor Descoudrelles, registered the following plantations and their owners:
- Morne Fortune (Pierre Desmonts)
- St. Jean (Jean Desmonts, born in Dutch-controlled South of St. Martin, son of P. Desmonts)
- Relief (Joseph Viellet de Chambery succeeded Claude Chabert as owner)
- St. James (James Lee, an Irishman from Cork, then a French, Dutch, and Danish subject)
- Concordia (John Heyliger and John Maillard associates, both from the Dutch-controlled South; J. Heyliger was a son of governor A. Heyliger; J. Maillard was of English origin)
- Diamant (Benjamin Gumbs, an Englishman from Anguilla who lived in the South of St. Martin)
- Gibraltar (sister-in-law of B. Gumbs)
- Sugarcane was also grown on Pierre Quary's property (four squares) and on Johannis Runnel's (four squares).

Development of Marigot quarter

The following are considered contributing factors to the gradual reduction in the number of sugar plantations in the Marigot Quarter:
- Consolidation of properties. It seems that the minimum profitable area consisted of fifty squares.
- The French Revolution, which sequestered six out of eleven plantations in Marigot, put a brake on further development at a time when the overall situation was promising for sugarcane planters.

Creole architecture, circa 1900, Backstreet 96. By F. de Kock. Courtesy: Sint Maarten Museum.

- Hurricanes: the most devastating of which came in 1772, 1792, 1819, and 1827.
- Poor soil and rain water shortage made the Lowlands less than ideal.

Of the eleven Marigot plantations, the ruins of St. Jean, Concordia, Diamant, Spring, and Lowlands *habitations* are still visible at the time of this writing.

The quarter's population

The Sugarcane Age of St. Martin was between 1770 and 1850. A local "aristocracy" was established by wealthy whites. The establishment was made up mostly of white planters and merchants, located in Great Bay (Philipsburg) or Marigot. They were chiefly of French, Dutch, or English origin, overwhelmingly Protestants (Dutch Reformist, Calvinist, and English Presbyterian). Catholics and Jews were among their numbers. The members of this class inter-married almost exclusively. They owned ships and engaged in the trade of human beings and goods, even after the slave trade was declared illegal by the European colonial powers. In 1808, Great Britain was the first of the European slave-trading nations to declare the trans-Atlantic slave trade illegal, followed that same year by the United States of America.

The St. Martin establishment leaders also supervised various plantations they owned on neighboring islands. They owned stores and warehouses on both sides of the island. The "aristocracy" had a lifestyle which ranged from modest, without immoderate luxury, to the excesses and evils common to slave plantations, which included rape, torture, dismemberment, murder, and selling of enslaved women, men, and children. (Old and crippled slaves who were unable to work were taken out to sea and drowned throughout the Caribbean.)

Inter-marriage between the wealthy white families that owned plantations in Marigot was commonplace. From the beginning, the Desmontses, Heyligers, Maillards, and Gumbses interwove family ties. Hardly any farmers or "poor" white landowners were found in the Marigot quarter. The destitute lived in non-sugarcane zones or in "Town," as Marigot's tiny center was called. The town started expanding around 1790. In "Town" were found craftsmen, fishermen, shopkeepers, and rat-catchers. Among this artisan group were Blacks, including mulattoes, who had been freed by

Bellevue sugar plantation ruins, by Cozbi Cabrera.

their masters, born of free parents, or had bought their own freedom and sometimes that of their children, parents, spouses, sweethearts, and others from the slave masters. Free Blacks appeared in more significant numbers most likely after the 1820s, and almost exclusively from the South of St. Martin, St. Eustatius, and Anguilla. It can be speculated that Maroons interacted with this group and that freedmen were among those murdered in Marigot by French authorities during the Revolt and Massacre of 1830.

The slave population on Marigot plantations increased considerably after 1772. The Black population from the Marigot plantations, "released" from slavery in 1795, numbered about nine hundred and forty persons around 1797. After the abolition of slavery in 1848, many newly-freed Black St. Martiners settled in St. James which was divided into lots. Hameau du Pont, made a distinct area from Concordia in 1850, was also settled by emancipated Blacks.

St. Jean plantation

The man who created St. Jean's plantation was probably Jean Desmonts, the owner in 1772. He was the widowed husband of Rebecca Gumbs who gave him a sole daughter, Ann Desmonts. He was a French Protestant, descendant of a Huguenot family that fled from religious prosecution in mainland Europe—first to London, then to the English colonies in the Caribbean. Later the Desmontses settled as rich merchants in the Dutch-controlled part of St. Martin.

Jean Desmonts's father, Pierre Desmonts, originally from Roergue, France, lived in the South of St. Martin and owned the Morne Fortune plantation in the Marigot Quarter. Desmonts was born in 1701, and must have been quite young when he fled with his family from France. While he was a merchant in Great Bay (Philipsburg), Pierre Desmonts's Morne Fortune plantation was at the very French/Dutch border on Simpson Bay Lagoon. A number of late eighteenth century reports about St. Martin note the great strategic value of the island with a large lagoon suitable for big ships and controlled by two colonial powers. In a time when France, England, and other nations waged a merciless war on the seas, merchants and seamen were often smugglers. The Desmonts family must have taken active part in the trade of human flesh and other cargo to and from the French- and Dutch-controlled parts of St. Martin, then to St. Eustatius, from where the "goods" were shipped to North America (thus evading English regulations during the war years).

The role of the Desmonts family in the evil slave trade and

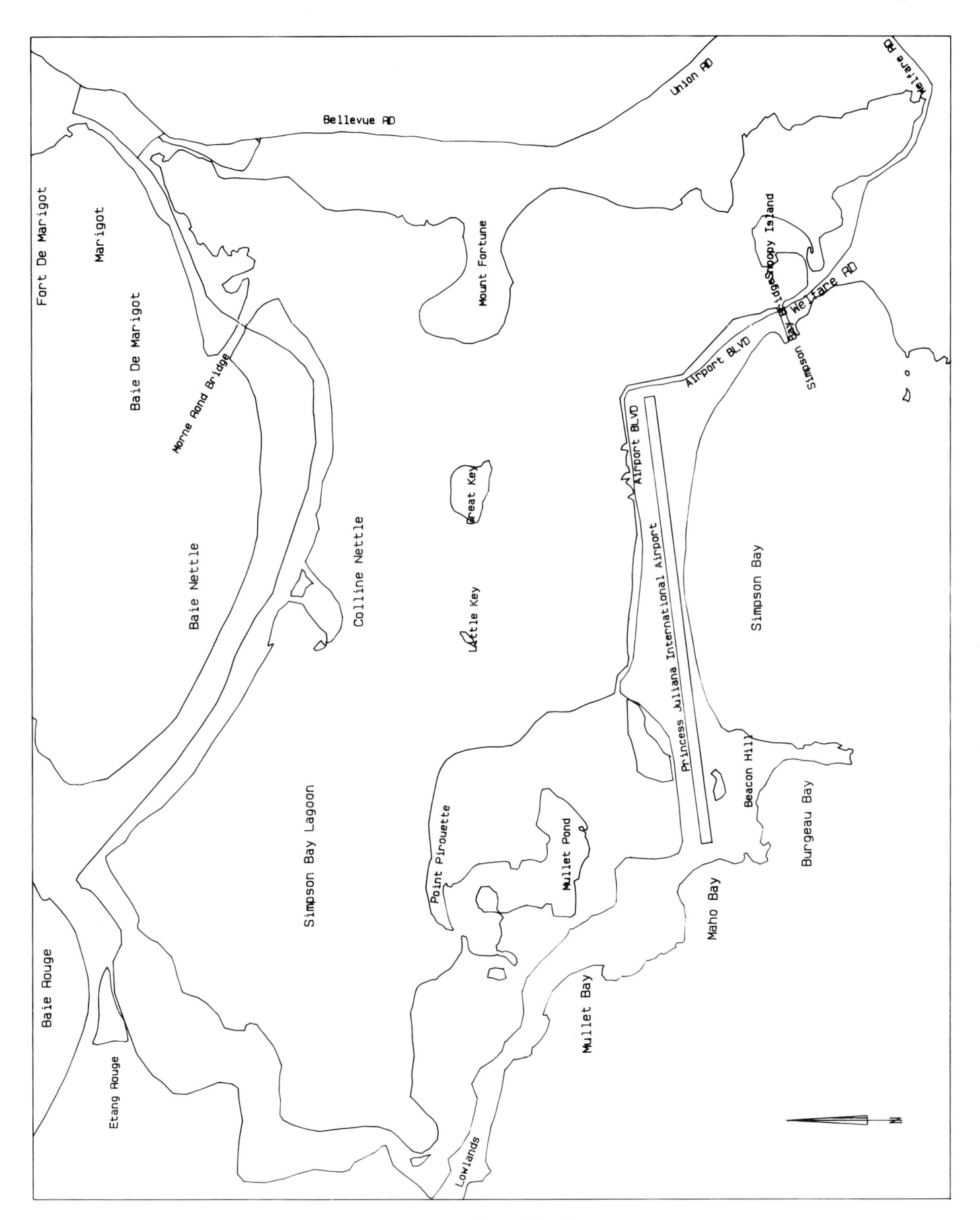

Source: Wing Surveys, 1996.

other contraband during the war years of the 1700s is inferred, if not evidenced by the "waste-cane deposit" on the property. This depository was located uncommonly far from the mill but very close to the lagoon shore. It had strongly barred windows, was well-bunkered, and the small "houses" up the hill overlooked the border and lagoon through their loopholes.

Ann and Sebastien de Durat

After Jean Desmonts died in 1777, his daughter Ann became his only heiress. She was still young when she married J. Doncker, of a Dutch merchant family settled in St. Eustatius and the South of St. Martin. Doncker died in 1786. Ann Desmonts, a widow, kept the estate running before she married her second husband, Sebastien de Durat. (It is thought that Sebastien is the same knight M. de Durat who was appointed governor of the French-controlled part of St. Martin in 1785, and who is credited in a 1833 report with having built Fort St. Louis and Hameau du Pont bridge in 1789. He belonged to a noble family which earned distinction in the French navy's exploits on the Caribbean Sea.) During the French Revolution, the plantation was confiscated. In 1801, the British invaded, and slavery was re-instituted. Ann was widowed again in 1814, and ran the estates with her children, Louis de Durat (mayor in Marigot from 1867 to 1871) and Lucette. The sugar mill was slightly damaged by the terrifying hurricane of 1819. Ann died in 1841, at age eighty.

The abolition of slavery

Slavery was abolished in St. Martin (North and South), Guadeloupe, Martinique, and the Danish colonies in 1848. Since 1820, the number of human beings imported as slaves had been steadily decreasing. A growing number of Maroons were "hiding out" among the free Black population and in isolated parts of the island, or had sailed away to the British colonies where abolition was enforced in 1833. In the French-controlled North, some planters and salt-pan owners, probably influenced by abolitionist and labor reformer Francois Perrinon and certainly because of the increasing number of Maroons and world market conditions, asked for the abolition of slavery in St. Martin in 1841.

At the dawn of emancipation, the Desmonts heirs owned three large sugar plantations south of Marigot town. The estates,

St. James, St. Jean, and Morne Fortune, were soon regarded as a single property. In St. James, the emancipated Blacks established a village. On the St. Jean *habitation* was a modest "master's house" and the best built sugar plant and mill on the island at that time. Louis de Durat supervised the family property until 1858. After his death, one of Ann's grandsons, John de Chalus, took over the running of the property. Its activities ceased in 1860.

The new owner became Louis-Alexandre von Romondt, of a merchant family from the Dutch-controlled South. The von Romondt family was very influential and active in Great Bay's political life and salt-works business. The family bought Bellevue Estate and most of the other plantations for sale in the French-controlled North. That is how Morne Fortune, St. Jean, and Bellevue estates became one contiguous property.

St. Jean plantation cemetery

The habit of burying people on their own property seemed to be quite common in St. Martin. This old-time custom might have started because Protestants were prohibited from burying their dead in the Catholic cemetery near the church (Enslaved Blacks were buried at the extremity of some plantations). The cemetery in St. Jean was marked by its sumptuousness due to the riches of the landlords. The St. Jean cemetery was located four hundred meters from the sugar mill, near a gully on the lower slopes (the running creek is thought to have undermined the mill building during flooding). The ruins of a funeral chapel with stonework walls was still standing at the time of the plantation survey. The oldest tombstone, of a baby, dated to 1808.

---

[13] *The same year of the slave uprising in Curacao led by the venerable Tula.*

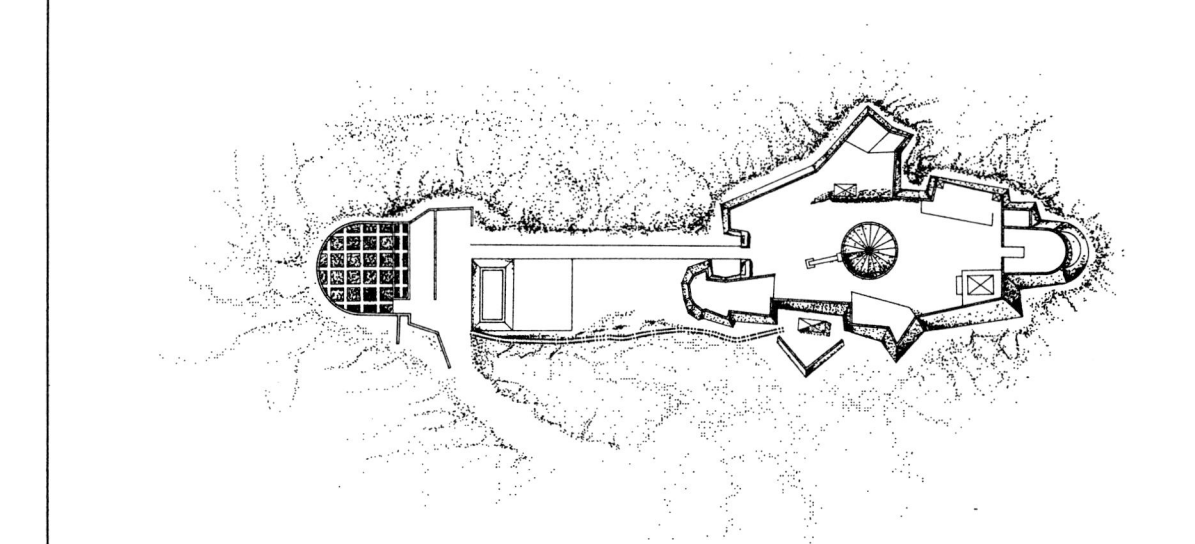

Plattegrond **Fort Willem**
Naar tekening van Sammuel Fahlberg omstreeks 1816.

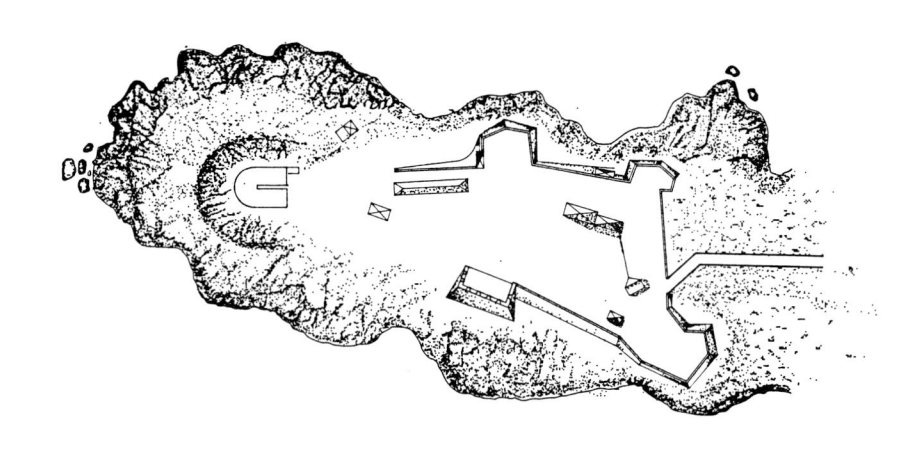

Plattegrond **Fort Amsterdam**
Naar tekening van Sammuel Fahlberg omstreeks 1816

Courtesy: PLAN'D2

FORTS OF ST. MARTIN

The capitals of St. Martin, Great Bay (Philipsburg) and Marigot, are strategically overlooked by forts. These forts were built centuries ago by slave labor to protect trade routes, commodities, and the newly coveted lands being exploited by the emerging European mercantile powers. From their hill-tops' vantage history can be imagined and wonderful views of "Sweet St. Martin" can be enjoyed.

Marigot, in the North of the island, is dominated by Fort St. Louis. Located above the harbor on a small hill, the fort, also called "Marigot Fort," commands the best view of the pretty city, Spring, Concordia, the northern reaches of Simpson Bay Lagoon, Sandy Ground, Lowlands, and neighboring Anguilla. To visit Fort St. Louis, walk or drive behind the Roman Catholic Church (built in 1842), pass the Marigot Hospital, and turn right into the Sous-Prefecture's parking-lot. From the parking-lot, a concrete stairway leads to the fort.

Fort St. Louis's powder-house and ruins of the defensive walls are still standing. A few cannons keep a lonesome vigil over land and sea. The Cultural and Historical Foundation of St. Martin often cleans the grounds. Built in 1737, Fort St. Louis is open to the public, day and night, at no charge. At night, floodlights enhance the outer walls which can be seen from the city below. In 1993, the French army used one of its helicopters to hoist two recovered cannons to the fort as part of on-going state-sponsored restorations.

Great Bay in the South had a more extensive defense system than Marigot. Two forts and two batteries defended the commerce, especially salt bound for the world market. The defensive system was put in place before the town was named Philipsburg, after John Philips, Lord of Almery-Clos. Philips, a reputedly brutal man, was commander for the South of St. Martin from 1734 to 1736, and again from 1737 until his death on December 17, 1746. He was fifty-eight years old.

The Bel-Air and St. Peter's batteries were demolished by modern development. The ruins of a cistern and house of St. Peter's battery are still visible on the other side of the Great Bay Marina on Juancho E. Yrausquin Boulevard. Bel-Air battery was built on the slope of Fort Hill with a clear cannon-shot view of Fort Amsterdam.

Fort Willem, at the peak of Fort Hill, dominates the western side of the capital. Broadcast and telecommunications towers rise above the fort's ruins. About half of St. Martin and all of the surrounding islands can be seen from Fort Hill on a clear day. At the time of this writing, a dirt road leads to the top, and erosion makes it dangerous for driving. A hike or "walk-up" can be adventurous. Start at the western extreme area of Great Bay Beach, cross Little Bay Road, and follow the dirt road to the fort. A slow walker will reach the top within an hour. Between 1801 and 1802, Fort Willem was called Fort Trigge by its British builders, under Commandant Robert Nicholson. Between 1802 and 1807, it was Fort Gelderland for the Dutch who chased away the British. From 1807 to 1810, the French reportedly captured the fort and called it Fort Louis Napoleon. The British recaptured the fort in 1810 and restored its first name before being driven off the island in 1816. That same year, under the Dutch occupation led by Commander Paulus Roelof Cantz'laar, Fort Willem I came to be.

Fort Amsterdam is historically the nation's most important fort. Positioned on the Little Bay Peninsula, Fort Amsterdam can be reached partly by car and on foot. Evolving from the 1631-32 fortifications, Fort Amsterdam is distinguished as one of the first European forts built in the Caribbean. In the nineteenth century, the fort ceased to be a military post. Up to the 1950s, a wireless signalling station existed within the fort's time-weathered walls, and since that time, a radio station's broadcast facilities laid within the historic ruins for a few years. Plans by Little Bay Beach Hotel owners to extend the hotel onto the peninsula resulted in its sale by the government in 1970. The Little Bay Beach Hotel's plans did not materialize, and the peninsula was sold several times thereafter. In 1987, Divi hotel corporation bought the peninsula and marched batteries of condominiums onto the peninsula. A large warehouse-looking structure was constructed within the fort's walls.

Conservation groups and concerned citizens have appealed to government and landowners to preserve the fort. The Fort Amsterdam Conservation Foundation has encouraged architectural and archaeological studies of the ruins to contribute toward restoring the fort as part of St. Martin's historical and labor patrimony and as a recreational site.

Old police station, Backstreet. Note officers and a bicycle near entrance.

A CHRONOLOGY OF ST. MARTIN'S FORTS

1629	The French build a small entrenchment in French Quarter.
1631/2	Jan Claesz van Campen, the first Dutch commander in the South of St. Martin, using enslaved African ancestors of today's St. Martiners, constructs a defense system on Great Bay Harbor's peninsula.
1633	Fifty-three Spanish warships and forty-two merchant marine vessels arrive to capture the island. After a week of fierce fighting, the Dutch and French surrender. The Spanish, under Governor Cibrian de Lizarazu, build a defense structure in the Pointe Blanche area and fortify the defense system on the peninsula. An average of three hundred people can occupy the fort.
1644	The Dutch, led by Peter Stuyvesant, try without success to recapture the fort from the Spanish. Stuyvesant loses his leg when his ship takes a direct hit from a Spanish cannon ball shot from the fort.
1648	The Spaniards, under Governor Diego Guajardo Fajardo, leave. Intolerable living conditions nearly cause the occupying soldiers to mutiny. One Black man is among the four Dutchmen and four Frenchmen said to have been hiding out on the island. Maroons, unrecorded, might also have been hiding from Spanish enslavers. Spanish return to Puerto Rico. On March 23, the French and Dutch settlers and colonial officials sign the Treaty of Concordia, vowing to "live as friends and allies."
1650	The British settle on Anguilla and try to capture St. Martin for the first time.
1737	Commander John Philips rebuilds "Fort St. Martin" and names it Fort Amsterdam after the Dutch West Indies Company's department of Amsterdam. The Dutch do not rebuild the fort to its former strength and size. The French may have started building fortifications atop Marigot Hill (future sight of Fort St. Louis).

St. Peter's battery is built in Pointe Blanche.	*1748*
The British gain control over fortifications atop Marigot Hill for two years.	*1781*
The British occupy parts of St. Martin.	*1784*
Fort St. Louis is built by the knight M. de Durat.	*1789*
The Dutch capture Fort St. Louis and control it for two years.	*1793*
The British return.	*1794*
The French recapture the island and control it for six years. Bel-Air battery is built. Slavery is discontinued by French Republicans.	*1795*
The British invade and occupy the island; reinstitute slavery, start to build Fort Trigge in the South, and are routed in 1802. Marigot is "surrendered" on January 24, 1803. French reinstitute slavery. British return in 1808.	*1801*
After being thrown out in 1808, the British return and control St. Martin for six years.	*1810*
The Dutch invade, regain control of Southern St. Martin and rename Fort Trigge, Fort Willem I. The French, battling the English since 1815, take control of the North under Baron de Proissi.	*1816*
Dutch Governor Johannes Willem van Romondt sends for additional troops in the wake of wide-spread resistance, escape, and sabotage by the enslaved population in the South of St. Martin. Slavery—already on decline before the 1834 emancipation in the Caribbean's British colonies—ceases in the North and South of St. Martin. (On July 1, 1863, slavery is abolished in the remaining Dutch colonies of the Caribbean.) Forts lose their military, judicial, and penal importance in St. Martin.	*1848*

HIGHEST HILLS

Paradise Peak, 424m

Mt. Careta, 401m

Mt. O'Reilly, 381m

Flagstaff, 391m

Sentry Hill, 341m

St. Peter's Hill, 316m

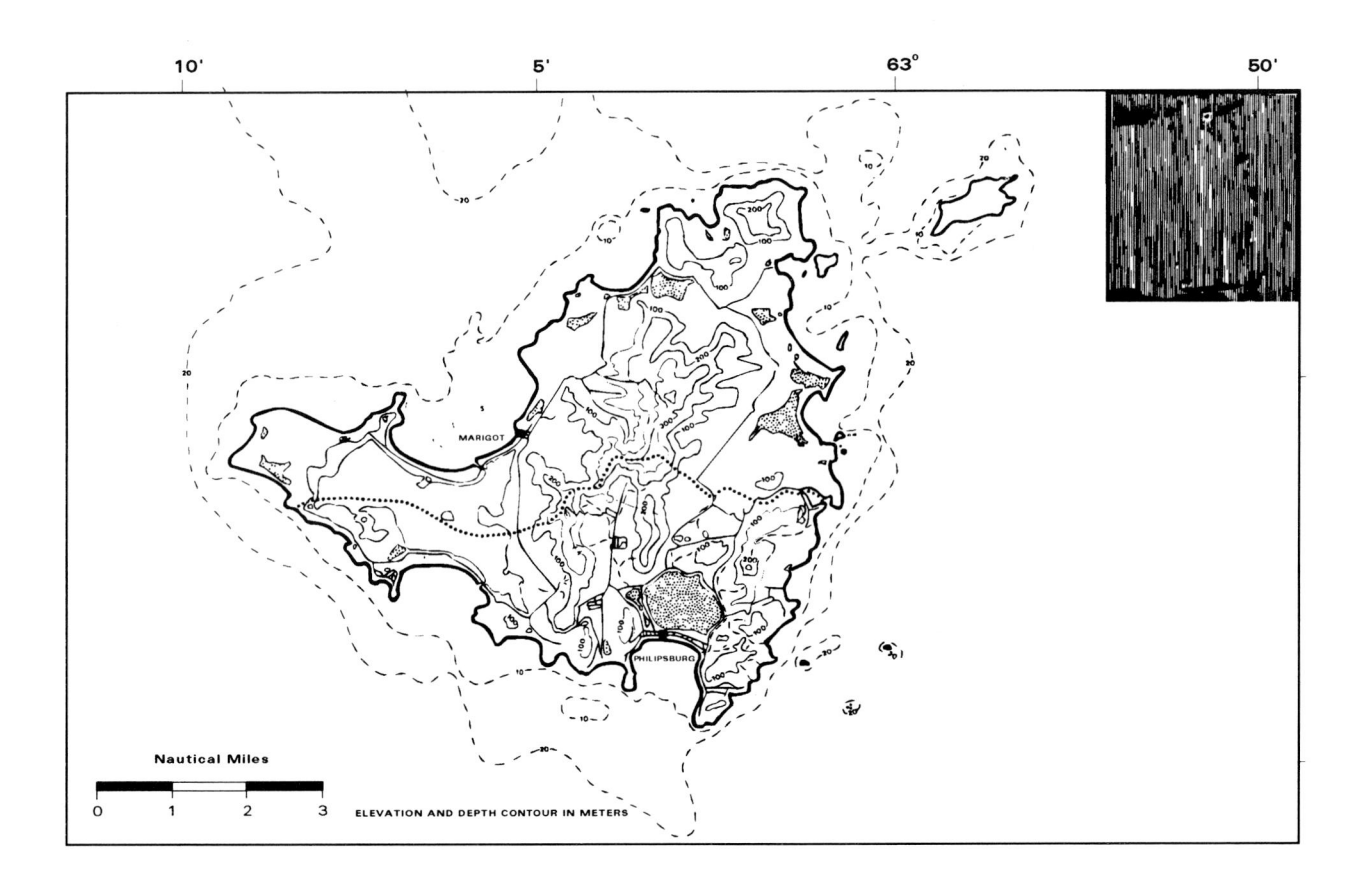

If you should still ask

why

it is because

...

...our ancestors

made history ... a sacred tradition.

— RAS CHANGA,
Because

MAP OF THE CARIBBEAN

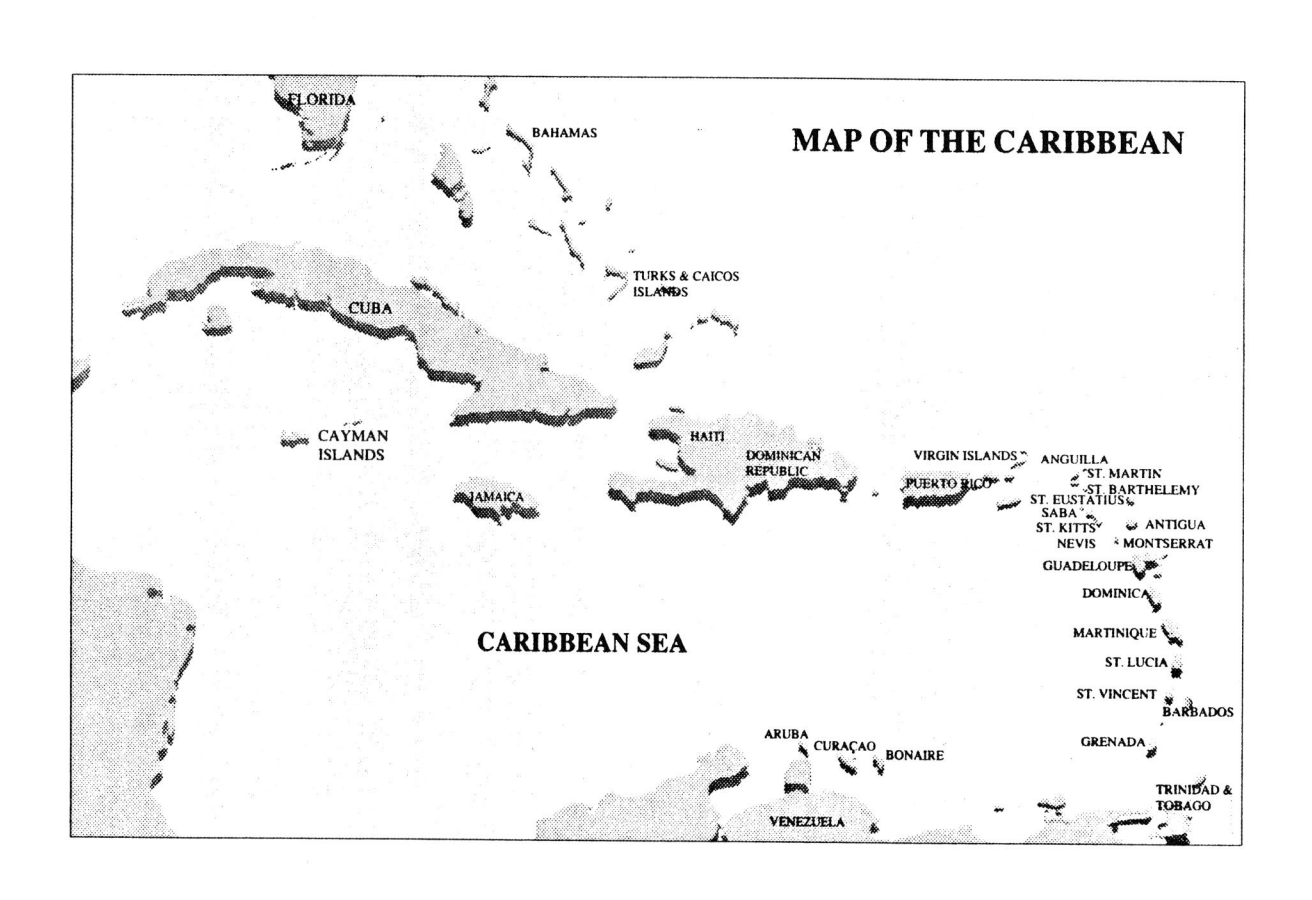

BIBLIOGRAPHY

Bibliographic Note

The material in this book is based on a large number of sources, among them the editor's own experiences, research, numerous writings, and interviews with publishers, political scientists, politicians, attorneys-at-law, historians, "older heads," educators, cultural workers, environmentalists, and family members and contemporaries of the personalities cited. This book is also the result of wide reading and research on St. Martin/Caribbean history, politics, culture, and natural environment. The following books, articles, and documents are among the basic sources consulted.

Arens, W. *The Man-Eating Myth – Anthropology & Anthropophagy*. New York: Oxford University Press, 1979.

Baly, Camille E. "Simartn – A People's History in Cultural Perspective." A paper presented at the St. Maarten Cultural Foundation's first celebration of St. Martin's Day, Curacao, 1991.

Barka, Norman F. "Archaeological Survey of Sites and Building, St. Maarten, Netherlands Antilles: I." St. Maarten Archaeological Research Series: No. 3 (1993): 32.

Benjamin, Ilva F., and Prince, Evelyn I. eds. "Illustrious Past, Challenging Future ... 1876-1976/Historical Perspective of Nursing in the U.S. Virgin Islands." Charlotte Amalie: Virgin Islands Nurses' Association, 1976.

Bobo, Nab Eddie. Letter to Lasana M. Sekou on Marie Richards's data search. 26 April 1993. House of Nehesi Publishers, St. Martin.

Bond, James. *Birds of the West Indies*. London: Collins, 1985.

Brooks, Rudy. "St. Martiner tells of 'murder' in nature's paradise." *St. Maarten/St. Martin Newsday*, 7-13 August 1992, p. 6, 8.

Bute, Ruby. *Golden Voices of S'maatin*. Philipsburg: House of Nehesi Publishers, 1989.

Changa, Ras. *Illegal Truth*. Philipsburg: House of Nehesi Publishers, 1991.

Campbell, Mavis C. *The Maroons of Jamaica – 1655-1796: A History of Resistance, Collaboration & Betrayal*. Trenton: Africa World Press, Inc., 1990.

Choisy, F. "Answer to Mr. L. C. Fleming." *Esprit De La Jeunesse*, 26 July 1947, p. 2.

_____. "Speech by Felix Choisy." *Windward Islands Opinion*, 10 March 1976, pp. 5, 4.

Consensus Populaire Saint-Martinois. *Saint-Martin – Ses Specificites, Ses Realites, Son Avenir*. Marigot: Consensus Populaire Saint-Martinois, (1992) [English edition, 1993].

Coomans, H. E., and Coomans-Estatia, M. *Flowers From St. Martin – The 19th Century Watercolours of Westindian Plants painted by Hendrik van Rijgersma*. Bloemendaal: De Walburg Pers, 1988.

Counter, S. Allen, and Evans, David L. *I Sought My Brother – An Afro-American Reunion*. Cambridge: MIT Press, 1981.

DCCA Environmental Fact Sheet No. 8. "Coastal Habitats: Mangroves." Charlotte Amalie: Eastern Caribbean Center, University of the Virgin Islands.

De Coste, Mercedes. Telephone Interview. 20 November 1993.

de Kock, Saskia. *Sint Maarten Historic Tour Guide.*" Philipsburg: Sint Maarten Museum, 1994.

"Drumming with J. H. Lake, Sr." *Shaka*, May 1974, pp. 5-8, 10, 14.

Duruo, Lorenzo. Telephone Interview. 21 November 1993.

"Editor's Desk." *Windward Islands Opinion*, 20 February 1973, p. 5.

Emery, Lynne Fauley. *Black Dance – From 1619 to Today*. London: Dance Books, 1988.

Encyclopedie van de Nederlandse Antillen, 2nd ed. (1985) S. v. "Gomez, Moises Frumencio da Costa," "Zout," "Bestuurders van de (Eislanden van de) Nederlandse Antillen."

Fenzi, Jewell. *This Is The Way We Cook (Asina Nos Ta Cushina) – Recipes From Outstanding Cooks of The Netherlands Antilles*. Willemstad: Thayer-Sargent Publications, 1978.

"For 'The Man Of The Week' We Nominate (Mr. Lionel Bernard Scott)." *W. I. Opinion*, 24 June 1961, pp. 1-2.

Fort Amsterdam Conservation Committee. "Fort Amsterdam Documentary Report 1986." Philipsburg: STINAPA, [1986].

Francis, Oswald. "Beaches you should visit on St. Maarten/St. Martin." *Welkom/Bienvenue St. Maarten/St. Martin*, (15-21) March 1993, p. 3.

Gibson, Richard F. "In Memoriam." *Windward Islands Newsday*, 23 March 1981, p. 2.

Glasscock, Jean. *The Making of an Island*. Massachusetts: (printed by) Windsor Press Inc., 1985.

"Grave of the Unknown Slave." *St. Maarten/St. Martin Newsday*, 31 August 1987, p. 10.

Greene, Cheryll Y., and Strickland, William. *Malcolm X: Make It Plain*. New York: Viking, 1994.

Gumbs, Esther. "Tales from the Great Salt Pond." Unpublished manuscript. 1995.

Haley, Alex. *The Autobiography of Malcolm X*. New York: Ballantine Books, 1965.

Harris, Robert; Harris, Nyota; and Harris, Grandassa. *Carlos Cooks and Black Nationalism from Garvey to Malcolm*. Dover: The Majority Press, 1992.

Haviser, Jay B., Dr. *In Search of St. Martin's Ancient Peoples – Prehistoric Archaeology*. Philipsburg: House of Nehesi Publishers, 1995.

Henocq, Christophe. "Le Fort Louis." *Bulletin Association Archéologique Hope Estate*, Edition 2 (1993): 10-14.

Heyliger, Cherra. "Miss Marie Richards – Nurse, Poet, Folklore Artist, Historian And Most Useful Citizen." *The West End News* (St. Croix, Virgin Islands), 1 October 1960, p. 4.

"Historical 'gold mine' found on St. Maarten/St. Martin." *St. Maarten/St. Martin Newsday*, 31 August 1987, p. 12.

Hodge, C. Borromeo, Jr. "José Lake, Sr. – The Man & The Hero." *St. Maarten/St. Martin Newsday*, 8-4 April 1994, pp. 2, 4-6.

_____. "Songs and Images of St. Martin." Unpublished manuscript. St. Martin, 1991

"Islets, Keys and Deserted Islands." *Discover St. Martin/St. Maarten*, 1991, pp. 69-76.

Jeffry, Daniella. "A Tribute to an Extraordinary Lady." *The St. Maarten Guardian*, 19 July 1989.

_____. "St. Martiners Know Your History." *St. Maarten/St. Martin Newsday*, 30 June 1983, pp. 9, 14, 16, 13.

Johnson, Will. *For the Love of St. Maarten*. New York: Carlton Press Inc., 1987.

Knappert, Jan. *The A-Z of African Proverbs*. London: Karnak House, 1989.

Knight, Franklin W. *The Caribbean – The Genesis of a Fragmented Nationalism*. New York: Oxford University Press, 1978.

Kruythoff, S. J., ed. *The Netherlands Windward Islands and a Few Interesting Items on French St. Martin – A Handbook of Useful Information for Visitor as well as Resident*. St. John: By the Author, The Excelsior Printery, 1938.

_____. *The Netherlands Windward Islands or Windward Group of the Netherlands Antilles – A Handbook of Useful Information for Visitors as well as Resident*. 3rd ed. Oranjestad: De Wit Inc., 1964.

Lafleur, Gerard. *Saint-Martin (Xviiie et Xixe Siecles) – Etude Socio-Economique de la Partie Française De Saint-Martin*. (Place, date of publishing not stated in 1980s publication).

Lake, Jr., Joseph H. "Plantation St. Maarten 120 years later." *St. Maarten/St. Martin Newsday*, 30 June 1983, pp. 20, 27.

Lake, (Sr.) Joseph H. The Lake Family Papers. Philipsburg, St. Martin.

Lamming, George. *Coming, Coming Home: Conversations II.* Philipsburg: House of Nehesi Publishers, 1995.

Lynch, Edgar, and Lynch, Julian. *Know Your Political History.* Philipsburg: Election Watchnite Association, 1990.

Martin, John Bartlow. *U.S. Policy in the Caribbean.* Boulder: Westview Press, 1978.

Mathurin, Lucille. *The Rebel Woman in the British West Indies during Slavery.* Kingston: Institute of Jamaica, 1975.

Netherlands Antilles Postal Service. "A Special Issue – Lionel Bernard Scott." Willemstad: Postal Service of the Netherlands Antilles, 1974.

Netherlands Antilles Supreme Court of Justice. Court Recorder. Philipsburg: Court Recorder. 1993.

"Paul Whit – A true St. Martin patriot passes on with a proud legacy." *St. Maarten/St. Martin Newsday,* 26 August/1 September 1994, p. 5.

Paula, A. F. *"Vrije" Slaven – Een sociaal-historische studie over de dualistische slavenemancipatie op Nederlands Sint Maarten (1816-1863).* Zutphen: Walburg Pers, 1993.

Perrinon, F. A. Letter to His Excellency, Mylord J. G. H. van Cets, van Gaudriaan, Minister of Interior Affairs, etc., etc., 20 August 1859. Municipal Library. Marigot, St. Martin.

Richardson, Evelyn. *Seven Streets by Seven Streets.* New York: Edward W. Blyden Press, 1984, pp. 26, 144.

Richardson, Joseph E. "1874-1949 Joseph Emmanuel Richardson – His Story of Saint Martin." *Discover St. Martin/St. Maarten,* 1986, pp. 63-77, 105.

Richardson, Lloyd. "Melford Hazel Celebrates 90th Birthday with Grand Family Reunion." *The Chronicle* (St. Martin), 6 July 1988.

_____. "The legendary 'Brother Bo' a. k. a. L. B. Scott." *The Chronicle* (St. Martin), 5 October 1987.

Saignes, Miguel Acosta. *Vida de los esclavos negros en Venezuela.* Valencia: Vadell Hermanos Editores, 1984, pp. 263-307.

Schiltkamp, J. A., Dr. and de Smidt, J. Th., Dr. *West Indisch Plakaatboek.* Vol. 3 Nederlandse Antillen Bovenwinden. *Publikaties en Andere Wetten Betrekking Hebbende op St. Maarten, St. Eustatius, Saba (1648/1681-1816).* Amsterdam: Dr. J. Th. de Smidt and Drs. T. van der Lee, 1979.

Sekou, Lasana M., ed. *National Symbols of St. Martin/St. Maarten – A Primer.* Philipsburg: House of Nehesi Publishers, 1990.

_____, gen. ed. *The Independence Papers. Vol. 1: Readings on a New Political Status for*

St. Maarten/St. Martin. Philipsburg: House of Nehesi Publishers, 1990.

_____. "Resistance to Slavery in St. Maarten." *St. Maarten/St. Martin Newsday*, 30 June 1983, pp. 20, 4, 17.

_____. "Stirring Gales at The Frontier – Charting a New Course, From St. Martin's Day to National Unification." *St. Maarten/St. Martin Newsday*. (Pt. 1) 27/3 November/December 1993, pp. 12, 11, 6; (Pt. 2) 4/10 December 1992, pp. 5-6, 11.

_____. "St. Martin & Political Destiny." *St. Maarten/St. Martin Newsday*. (Pt. 1) 17/23 June 1994, pp. 12, 11; (Pt. 2) 1/7 July 1994, pp. 12, 3, 4, 8-10.

Sint Maarten Museum Foundation. "First Exhibit 1989: Forts of Sint Maarten/Saint Martin." Philipsburg: Sint Maarten Museum Foundation, 1989.

Six, Diedrik, L., ing. "Study on Fort Amsterdam." Commissioned Study, Divi Little Bay Hotel, St. Martin, 1990 (Typewritten).

Solien-Gonzalez, Nancie. *Black Carib Household Structure – A Study of Migration and Modernization*. Seattle: University of Washington Press, 1980.

"Sons of the Soil featured in Marcus Garvey Exhibit." *St. Maarten/St. Martin Newsday*, 14 August 1987.

"Sugar Plantations of Saint Martin." *Discover St. Martin/St. Maarten*, 1992, pp. 37-39.

"Survey of Conservation Priorities in the Lesser Antilles – Saint Martin/Sint Maarten Preliminary Data Atlas." The Eastern Caribbean Natural Area Management Program. Caribbean Conservation Association et al., 1980.

"SXM Garveyites to get special honor this evening." *St. Maarten/St. Martin Newsday*, 17 August 1987, pp. 1, 3, 10.

Sypkens Smith, M. P. *Beyond the tourist tap: A study of Sint Maarten Culture*. Amsterdam: Foundation for Scientific Research in the Caribbean Region: 136. 1995.

Teenstra, M. D. *The Islands of the Netherlands West Indies: St. Maarten*. Tropical Mirror Series of reprints on the history of St. Maarten in the Netherlands Antilles. Translated from Dutch by John W. Philipsen. Philipsburg: Lord & Hunter, 1993.

The Direction. "About A Monument." *Esprit De La Jeunesse*, 13 March 1948, pp. 1-2.

Van der Hoeven, F., and Vliegen, J. Educational Letter Number 2. "Sint Maarten Beaches." Philipsburg: STINAPA [1983].

Vliegen, J. Educational Letter Number 1. "Brown Pelicans." Philipsburg: STINAPA [1983].

_____. Educational Letter Number 3. "Sint Maarten Ponds." Philipsburg: STINAPA [1983].

_____. World Environment Day – Sint Maarten. "Trees." Philipsburg: STINAPA et al., [1982].

"Wallace laid to rest." *Windward Islands Newsday*, 23 March 1981, p. 1.

Waymouth, J. C. *Memories of Saint Martin (Netherlands Part) – 1522-1926*. Philipsburg: Self-published.

Zinn, Howard. *A People's History of the United States*. New York: Harper Perennial, 1980.

"1848 - 1948." *Esprit De La Jeunesse*, 8 May 1948, pp. 1-3.

INDEX

Africa, 79, 110, 138, 146
American Embargo Act, 147
Anguilla, 34, 35, 76
"Antillean Personality," 58
Arawak, 135
Arndell, Jocelyn, 75
Aruba, 63, 96
Ashanti, 146
Bahamas, 112
Baly, Camille, 10, 70, 72, 138
Baly-Lewis, Inez Eliza, 49
Bamboulley, 37
Beaujon, J. "Jappa," 51, 71
Black Star Line, 65
Bobo, Nab Eddie, 62, 90
Bonaparte, Napoleon, 41, 147
Bradshaw, Robert L., 76
Brazil, 29, 139
British Emancipation Act, 34, 42
Brouwer, Anthony R., 51
Brown pelican, 15, 133-136
"Bush Lawyer," 83
"Buy Black," 61, 62
Caribs, 30, 134
Certificat d'Etudes, 101
Chatoyer, 134
Choisy, Felix, 56, 67, 71
Christian Democratic Party, 74
Concordia, 101, 102
Congo, 61, 146
CONSENSUS, 11
Cooks, Carlos, 39, 60
Cooks, James Henry, 64, 95
Cotton, 146
Council
   - General, 87
   - Island, 68, 71, 97
   - Municipal, 101
Court of Policy (Raad van Politie), 52, 96

Cuba, 139
Curacao, 47, 52, 69, 96
De Slag om Slag (Blow by Blow), 52
Democratic Party
   - St. Croix, 91
   - St. Martin (North), 56, 103
   - St. Martin (South), 69, 70, 84, 94
Descoudrelles, Augustin, 145
Desmontses, 150
Dessalines, Jean-Jacques, 41
Diamond Estate 26, 45
Dominica, 30, 135
Dominican Republic, 60, 63, 76, 95
Duncan, Roland, 70, 81
Duruo, Thomas E., 63, 95, 102
Dutch East India Company, 110
Emancipation, 35, 40, 42, 57
"Emancipation Song," 15, 47
Espirit De La Jeunesse, 56, 103
Famine of 1809, 147
Federal Bureau of Investigation
   (FBI), 61
Fleming, Elie, 87
Fleming, Louis Constant, 56
Forts, 154-159
France, *vii*, 42, 57, 145, 150
Friday, Leo, 71
Friday, Raphael, 93
Garifuna, 134
Garvey, Marcus Mosiah, 60, 68
General Workers Union, 81
Ghana, 61
Gibson, Richard, 9, 84
Gomez, da Costa Moises F., 73, 97
Great Bay, 3, 143, 155
Grenada, 34
Guadeloupe, 57, 78, 87
Guavaberry, 16, 139
Guinea, 146
Gumbs, Louis Crastell, 109

Guyana, 135
Habitations de la Republique, 147
Haiti, 41
Hameau du Pont, 150
Hazel, Melford Augustus, 68, 97
Herald (St. Croix), 90
Holland (The Netherlands), *vii*, 42, 110
Hurricanes, 3, 96, 121, 123, 147
India, 140
IOAC, 65
Jackson, David Hamilton, 90
Jamaica, 31, 65, 146,
James, Vance Jr., 94
"Jeagro," 71
Jeffry, Daniella, 36, 79, 100
Johnson, Will, 65, 98
"July Tree," 15, 47
Jumbies, 140
King, Martin Luther Jr., 86
LAGO, 65, 75, 82
LAGO Employee Council, 75
LAGO Employee Council News, 75
Lake, Joseph Husurell Jr., 32, 71, 76, 97, 108
Lake, Joseph (José) Husurell Sr., 58, 70, 93
Lamming, George, *v*, 145
Larmonie-Duverly, Nina, 78
Lohkay, One-Tété, 32, 38
Lumumba, Patrice, 61
Marcus Garvey Centennial Award, 67, 69
Marigot, 31, 36, 78, 148
Maroons, 29-34
Maroon nations, 30
Martinique, 36, 79
National Flag of St. Martin, 4-7
Nationale Volkspartij (NVP), 69, 71, 97

Netherlands Antilles (The), 69, 75, 97
Newsday, St. Maarten/St. Martin, 74
Nkrumah, Kwame, 61
Non-intercourse Act, 147
NWIWA (St. Marten Club), 75
Opinion, Windward Islands, 70, 81, 96
Oranje Benevolent Improvement Association (OBIA), 69
Oranje School, 60, 71
Order of Oranje-Nassau, 98
Ordre National du Merite, 101
Ouatouba, 37
Palmeres, 30
Paris Society for the Abolition of Slavery, 79
Partido Patriotico Arubano (PPA) 73
Perrinon, Francois Auguste, 79
Persona non grata, 70
Peters, Alrett Bertraund, 81
Peterson, Wallace Bradford, 83
Petit, Hubert, 58, 70, 87
Petronia, Ernesto, 72
Philippe, Louis, 35, 36
Philipsburg, 3, 115, 155
Philipsburg Mutual Improvement Association (PMIA), 96
Plantations, 145
Ponum dance, 15, 47, 49
Powell, Adam Clayton, 61
Puerto Rico, 43
Pump drum, 47, 50
Red Cross, 90
Referendum (St. Maarten), 34
Revolutions
 - French, 34, 36, 41, 57, 146
 - Haitian, 31, 36, 146
Richards, Alberic Áurelien, 86
Richards, Marie, 90

Richardson, Joseph Emmanuel, 35
Richardson, Leonides, 93
Roumou, Wilfred, 19, 39, 76
Salt ponds
- novelties, 113
- production, 38, 110-118
- socialization in, 42
San Pedro de Macoris, 64
Scott, Lionel Bernard, 67, 95
Seaview Hotel, 68
Sequestre, 41, 147
Simpson Bay Lagoon, 124, 150
Slavery
- abolition, 40-45, 79, 152
- laws, 32, 34, 41
- rebellion, uprising, 35, 41
- torture, 38, 39, 149
- trade, 4, 108, 149
SMAFESTAC, 49
SMECO, 8, 58, 104
Spain, 42
Statuut of 1954, 97
St. Croix, 43, 70, 90
St. Eustatius, 34, 81, 96, 150
St. James, 150
St. Martin
- beaches, 126-129, 132
- birds, 121
- drinks/liquers, 16
- festivals/holidays, 15
- flora, 5, 130-132, 142
- foods, 16
- fruits, 17
- hills, 160
- keys, 132
- lagoon, 124, 150
- mangroves, 122
- monuments, 16
- Motto, 4, 58
- population, 3, 147, 150
- sayings/proverbs, 18
- trees, 15, 138-142
St. Thomas, 69
St. Vincent, 30, 135
Sualouiga, 3,
Tanny and The Boys, 139
"The Village," 65
Tobacco, 146
Ton'ton Butty, 140
Treaty of Concordia, 6, 15, 29, 36, 57, 115
Trinidad, 34, 35, 38, 135
United People's Liberation Front, 74-75
Universal Negro Improvement Association, 60, 63, 76, 95
Universal Suffrage, 73, 91
Van Romondts, 45, 47, 111
Venezuela, 31
Venter-Trott, Simeone, 100
Wara-wara, 94
Wathey, Claude, 13, 70, 71, 97
West Indies Company, 110, 115
Whit, Paul Sr., 56, 102
Windward Islands Peoples Movement, 75
X, Malcolm, 61

Rhoda Arrindell and Lasana M. Sekou. Photo/L. Bharath.

LASANA M. SEKOU is the author of nine books of poetry, monologues, and short stories. In 1990, he edited *The Independence Papers*, St. Martin's first compilation of political essays, with O. Francis and N. Gumbs. In 1991, he was the executive producer for *Fête – The First Recording of Traditional St. Martin's Festive Music* by Tanny & The Boys. A number of Sekou's articles on history, culture, and politics have appeared in St. Martin's *Newsday* (for which he has been an editor since 1984). He is interviewed regularly by Caribbean, American, and European print and broadcast media on St. Martin/Caribbean history, culture, and politics. His poetry and reviews of his writings have appeared in *Discover St. Martin-St. Maarten*, *The Caribbean Writer*, *Del Caribe*, *The Massachusetts Review*, *De Gids*, *Revue Noir*, and other regional and international journals and magazines. Sekou holds a B.A. in political science/international relations, State University of New York at Stony Brook; and an M.A. in mass communications, Howard University.

RHODA ARRINDELL is a linguist and lecturer in English-as-a-second language at the University of St. Martin. From 1989 to 1992, Arrindell was an editor for *The Progressive*, the news and information organ of St. Martin Educational & Cultural Organization. A member of the St. Martin Independence Foundation, Arrindell holds a B.A. from Syracuse University. The mother of one daughter works as copy editor for one of the nation's daily newspapers, and was the editorial assistant on this book.